UNEXPECTED GRACE

When Your Child is Born with Half a Heart

Annie B. Garman

Scripture quotations are from The ESV® Bible (The Holy Bible, English
Standard Version®), copyright © 2001 by Crossway, a publishing ministry of
Good News Publishers. Used by permission. All rights reserved.

ISBN: 0692606386
ISBN 13: 9780692606384
Library of Congress Control Number: 2015921091
Annie B. Garman, Triangle, VA

To Gracie and Noel

It's because of you that this story is being told

TABLE OF CONTENTS

PREFACE

On August 18th, at 3:30 in the morning, I got this wild idea to record the story you're about to read.

It was an alloy of motives that prompted me to begin documenting this story. I was completely clueless to what it would require of me, and surely over-confident in my writing ability. But, more than anything, I wanted to point everyone within earshot to the God that I served. I felt like maybe God had brought me into this world of heart defects to be an ambassador for Him. I wanted the world to see and know the faithfulness of God, even in the midst of a trial.

Little did I know, *this would not be so easy...*

The writing process revealed things in my heart that were hard to admit to myself, let alone write down and record for all to see. I began to see just how brittle my faith was, how immature my reactions were, *and how weak my words were to communicate it all.* As I began to document everything I was experiencing, it brought up questions that I wasn't sure I knew how to answer. It made me question so many things I had always just believed.

Throughout the past five years, I've given up writing this book many times. *People have been through MUCH harder things and handled them MUCH BETTER. Can my words really help anyone? This story will never be a best seller...why waste my time and energy? I'm not sure I **want** people to know my thoughts and emotions during this time...is it really helpful to share them?*

Even though I still don't have all the answers to those questions, I invite you to embark through my thoughts and emotions in the following pages. Each chapter begins with a verse that God used during this critical time and each page is simply what I recorded during this journey. It's my prayer that, *as I show you a little more of who I am (weak, flawed, prideful, brittle, etc.)*, **God would show you a little more of who He is**.

He is faithful and He is good.

I had heard...but now I have seen.

"Let this be recorded for a generation to come, so that a people yet to be created may praise the Lord."

Psalms 102:18

PROLOGUE

November 27th, 2009
Reykjavik, Iceland

It wasn't a dream that woke me. It was fear, cold and black.

I sat up straight in bed as the night split wide open with anxiety. Disoriented, I groped around until I felt the wall to my right. I gulped down air, panic shaking my body like a cold chill.

God, I'm so scared. I could never handle it. What if it happens to me?

Just last year I had heard the news when we were living in Finland. I had turned up the music loud, real loud on my ipod and gone for a run because I didn't know what else to do...What *else* can one do?

I had cried, nearly screamed at God out in the Scandinavian forest where no one could hear me. *Please, God. Save him... He's only two! You can HEAL HIM, JESUS. We need a miracle from You! Oh God, please, kill the tumor. Jesus, I know you CAN... but will you? You're the only hope we have...*

The trees were tall and they barely swayed in response, unaffected. Cold hearted.

And just last night I had read the end of the story.

He was gone. There was nothing they could do. He was only two years old.

The brave parents, our dear friends, Summer and Jeremy, were weathering the ultimate storm. I was sick for them... sick for myself. *I could never get pregnant again;* that was the only application to this message. *It was too risky.* I had gone to bed with a tense stomach and body.

I now sat up in bed, unable to see even my hands shaking in front of my face. My husband lay next to me, sleeping obliviously, warm and calm. I scooted over closer to him, his warmness melting me, relaxing my breathing. Just feeling him near.

We had been trying to have a third child for many months and I was at a crossroads. Could we really get pregnant again with this tragedy so fresh--so raw? There was nothing else I wanted but another child, yet fear was body slamming me, pinning me down... and chasing me away all at the same time.

I sat close to my husband's sleeping body and God brought Summer's words to my mind. "I imagine Tyson running through the pearly gates, and God saying, "Well done, thy good and faithful servant."

God, I want to trust you...I want to have another child, but I'm so scared. Please give me courage to trust you. Please give us a child and help us to entrust this child—YOUR CHILD-- to you... for your purposes.

My breathing relaxed even more. My shaking arms began to go limp at my side as I pictured Jesus holding me. Then I must have fallen asleep.

I think I was already pregnant.

1

LUCKY NUMBERS

*"For I consider that the sufferings of this present time
are not worth comparing with the glory that is to be
revealed to us."*

Romans 8:18

March 29th, 2010
Reykjavik, Iceland

The alarm went off and I rolled over into my husband's arms before even opening my eyes. A ray of Icelandic sun pierced through the window at just the right angle, tugging at my heavy eyelids and prodding them to open. It had been a long, dark winter and I laid still thinking of how pleasant it felt to finally rise with the sun. Soon there would be sunlight for twenty-one hours of the day, but for now it felt normal, like home in Virginia.

"Are you excited?" my husband, Colby, asked softly after a few moments of quiet.

"Not really..." I responded rather groggily, the morning robbing my ability to filter my words.

"What are you talking about?" Colby looked offended as he tried to sit up in bed. "We get to find out *what it is* today."

"I don't want to go..." I explained, "...I don't want to find out what's wrong."

Colby let out a loud laugh that said, *"You're so pessimistic, it's unbelievable,"* then paused rather abruptly mid-laugh as though he was considering what it would feel like if my intuition was right.

"Well, if something **is** wrong, wouldn't you want to know about it?" he processed out loud after a few moments of silence.

"No... **Absolutely not.** *I'd rather not know.* I don't want to go through the pain of finding out." He shook his head at my logic and I just shrugged as I got out of bed, not even sure *I* was following my train of thought.

My pessimism wasn't rooted in illogical fear, but rather in realism. We had waded in enough waters of death in recent months. I had recently suffered a miscarriage, Tyson had just passed away from a brain tumor, and our friend had been killed in Afghanistan by a roadside bomb. I could feel cynicism starting to knock on the door of my heart.

I felt like vomiting as my feet hit the floor, but after drinking some water, burping, and going to the bathroom, the nausea passed.

"Mommy, my pants arwe twangled..." I followed the voice of my three year old to her room where she was sitting on the ground, wrestling a pair of thermal underwear. "Good morning, Darcy," I smiled at her head full of curls, wild from the night.

As I bent down to help her, I reached over with my spare hand to ruffle the hair of my five year old, still in bed. She opened her eyes and I was nearly blinded by the blue. Looking into Haley Jane's eyes was like looking directly into the sun.

"Haley Jane....it's time to get up," I whispered, knowing how she felt. "Do I have to wear my thermals today?" The first words out of her mouth.

"Yes. Every day. You know this." We had the same conversation every morning.

"But, do I have to wear the WOOL sweater over it?" The blue was getting wet at the very mention of it.

"Well...I guess you can find some *other* sweater to put over it...but you know you'll have recess outside today."

A school worker had informed me that the children would go outside for recess every day, the only exception being a wind so strong that it prevented the children from standing in an upright position. That occasionally happened.

We moved quickly through the breakfast routine, but didn't bother clearing the table. If we didn't move fast, we would miss the bus and have to walk to school. Colby took Darcy and I took Haley each to their different schools.

The whole morning butterflies were dancing wildly inside of me. Everything felt different this time, but not in a good way. It was different *in that I felt my luck running out.* We had always rolled good numbers, but the dice couldn't keep going in our favor forever.

Down the street at our Icelandic class, Colby and I filled our notebooks with Icelandic nouns, and then used those new words to help read a short story. I nibbled on an apple the entire time. After class we packed our backpacks like schoolchildren, and walked hand in hand to Landspítali, the Icelandic clinic, where we took our seats in a small waiting room.

A pregnant teenage girl came in with her family and what looked like her boyfriend. *Why me and not her?* I wondered. I had to turn my head to stop myself from staring at her and her giddy partner that I was growing to despise. I had no grounds to be thinking such awful thoughts. *Maybe I'm just being pessimistic.* The teenager looked at a magazine, oblivious.

Our name was called and we went back.

I never wanted to have children.

I never wanted to get married, at least that's what I claimed. I met Colby John Garman my freshman year of college outside the post office on campus. He was wearing a plastic bow tie (obviously attained from a staff member at the nearby dollar theatre) and he shook my hand stiffly and jovially as though he was pretending to be a politician. I can remember the morning sun being in my eyes as I looked at him and could really only make out a fuzzy silhouette.

As the year progressed, I could hardly go ten feet without running into Colby. Convocation, cafeteria, ministry team practice, religion hall...our interests and activities overlapped to such an extent that a day in the life of Annie was never spent without some portion of Colby.

He gave me all his notes and helped me get through Theology 202 with Dr. Morrison; I helped him practice rhythm on his guitar. I cut his hair; he taught me how to lighten mine with hydrogen peroxide. We played together in the rain during a flashflood, listened to Caedmon's Call in the Laundromat, and talked about the timeline of Western Civilization over lunch.

Whenever I had a question about something I read in the Bible, Colby was the first person I called. He had just become a Christian and had switched his major from Business to Biblical studies. He was brilliant and I wanted to glean everything I could from him. By the end of the year we were best friends although we had never told each other that.

The day Colby asked me out, I buried my face in my hands and groaned, asking him why he was trying to ruin such a good thing.

Commitment was scarier to me than death, really. How could I settle down in a serious relationship when I was only nineteen? Didn't he realize the ramifications of such a decision? I had a world to travel and conquer, and I did not (did *not*) want marriage to hinder me. I wanted to be free to do as I pleased, without having to consider another person (quite possibly the *very* definition of selfishness).

I wasn't interested in a relationship, so I figured that meant I had lost my best friend. Surely Colby would move on to wooing another woman with his intellect and charm and drop me like a bad habit.

My sophomore year marched on, but Colby was still everywhere I turned. The funny thing was, he acted like my rejection of him had never happened. We would sit outside the library on the dirty, old couches and talk about the history of the English language, Old Testament law, ecclesiology, and world missions until curfew. He still made me laugh so hard that I would fall off the couch and slap the carpet in a fit of exuberance.

My roommates would roll their eyes when I came into the room at midnight, face flushed with laughter and heart full. *"You like him..."* they would say as they turned off their reading lights and laid down on their bunk beds. I would get defensive and angry, my conflicted heart not so sure of what was happening. "I do NOT like him. WE. ARE. JUST. FRIENDS. Can't two people just be friends?" They didn't bother arguing...

Having Colby's friendship during that season was beginning to heal my heart in ways I didn't even know it needed. He had wisdom beyond his years and having him in my life was like having my personal therapist/pastor/professor.

Throughout the next year, as our friendship continued to blossom, Colby would occasionally muster up the courage to *casually* ask if I was interested in being in a relationship yet. I couldn't believe the guy. He had persistence and nerve like no one I'd ever met. Wasn't one rejection good enough for him? Surely he wasn't understanding. My indecisiveness was so problematic that I frequently caused back-ups at Dunkin' Donuts and other such organizations. Fear of commitment ran deep.

I would tell him no. In an effort to not be so harsh, I would assure him that we could be *neighbors* the rest of our lives...but I really didn't think we had a future beyond that. He would say okay, and then we would carry on like nothing had happened.

Looking back, it was a miracle of God that He was able to change my heart. And by *He*, I mean God of course.

2

BALANCE

"When you pass through the waters, I will be with you; and through the rivers, they shall not over-whelm you; when you walk through fire you shall not be burned, and the flame shall not consume you."

Isaiah 43:2

March 29th, 2010
Reykjavik, Iceland
1:15 pm

I heaved my heavy body onto the cold hospital bed. Still a little numb from the Icelandic wind, I could feel goose bumps explode all over my body. It was the long-awaited twenty-week ultrasound and I was nervous.

For this pregnancy, we had decided to find out the gender for ourselves but not tell anyone else. It would be our little secret so we could get organized, but everyone else would have to endure the suspense.

I felt shaky as the midwife put on the gel and started the camera. The image of our baby's spine appeared almost immediately on the screen. It was nothing short of miraculous to see **life** moving and kicking *from the inside out,* and I just watched for a long time with tears streaming down my face. *It's alive. Thank you God. I was wrong...it's alive.*

Our friends in Virginia had just had two miscarriages in a row. Because of this, I had hesitated to get excited for this pregnancy. There was just so much that could go wrong...

"We're still working on our Icelandic, so is it okay if we do this sonogram in English?" my husband asked and the midwife nodded.

She wasn't very talkative, so I laid in cold and silence while she clicked on her computer, measuring the length of the femur and taking pictures of our baby's profile. Even though they were very kind, the reservedness of Icelanders always made me wonder if I had done something wrong. I remembered my last ultrasound in Virginia and how jovial the room felt as we all laughed, chatted, and loudly commented on everything we were seeing.

I watched her serious eyes and thought, regardless of the stoicism, how fortunate we were to live in a country where most people were very proficient in English. We had been living in Iceland for over a year, working hard to learn the language and start a Baptist church. Nothing about it had been easy, but at least we could "cheat" and speak in English with most people when we needed to.

"Did you say that you wanted to know the gender?" she asked with her thick Icelandic accent.

We looked at each other as though we were still considering our decision. It HAD been fun to be surprised with the gender of Darcy at her birth. I sighed. *We needed to find out.* Having a baby in a different country was going to add enough stress as it was. I nodded.

"I hear you already have two little girls at home," she said to Colby as she looked at her screen. He nodded. She turned to him, a smile cracking. "Well, you're about to have one more."

Colby broke out into a grin as he looked down at me.

"I thought that's what that was," he said through his smile.

I looked up at him with a face of bewilderment. Since when could he decipher genders on an ultrasound? We locked eyes for a long time, smiling and exchanging quiet *I-can't-believe-its.*

I was shocked. Elated. Confused (why had I been so much sicker this time?). Giddy with excitement. I laid and looked at the ceiling, while visions of frills and bows danced through my head; I couldn't believe I got to do all of it again.

My dreaming was cut short. The midwife's face changed and her smile disappeared. *Was this normally how she acted or was something wrong?* I couldn't tell and my breathing started to change. It started to feel shallow and short. Finally she spoke.

"I'm not seeing everything I need to see here in the four chambers of the heart."

Sixty seconds.

It couldn't have been any more time than that. No more than a minute to celebrate before my heart dropped. I held my breath and stared hard at the midwife, wondering if I was dreaming or not. It felt ....like the floor our feet were jumping and celebrating on had cracked and I was falling through.... like a touchdown that was called back after the crowd had gone wild...

She left the room and Colby continued his celebration. "I *knew* it. *I knew I was going to have all daughters.*"

I looked up at him, *absolutely astonished* that he wasn't thinking what I was thinking. "She has a *heart defect,*" I said, not sure if I totally believed it, but wanting instead to see how he'd react to my cynicism.

He rolled his eyes. "That's not what she said. She's *just* a midwife. She can't see everything she needs to see to release us, but after the doctor sees it… *then we can go home.* I'm sure this happens all the time." He was still smiling, the celebration fresh on his face.

I couldn't believe how naïve and positive he was being. I hoped he was right, but I knew he wasn't.

And then I started weeping uncontrollably.

He looked completely confused. The more hysterical I became, the more he began to see that his reassurance was worthless. I buried my face in his chest and grieved for something that hadn't yet happened…while Colby's own celebration faded into oblivion.

We were ushered through what felt like a rabbit hole, down flights of stairs, past different wards, up hallways, and through heavy doors until we arrived at the Cardiology ward. The pediatric cardiologist said very little as he put the gel on my stomach.

Two minutes passed.

The clock on the wall stood as still as our breath. The doctor's large hand—bracing my stomach to get an image–moved ever so slightly with each pound of my heart. He held on tight, like riding a rollercoaster over my nerves.

Four minutes.

Four and a half.

I stared at the ceiling and focused on one particular spot like you're supposed to do when balancing on a beam.

Five minutes.

I listened to time pass. The future was screaming like a train whistle...screaming so loud that I almost couldn't hear. Screaming so loud that it almost didn't seem real.

Six minutes.

This can't be good, I thought loudly. *If everything was just fine, he would have said so by now. We would be smiling, shaking hands and leaving...going home to tell our daughters that they have a new sister.*

Eight minutes.

I watched my husband out of the corner of my eye. He was straining to see. Straining to understand an ultrasound only a cardiologist can decipher. He bit his bottom lip ever so slightly and I stared long, wondering if his faith was shaking as hard as my body.

He looked down at me. A wink. A squeeze. They didn't reassure.

Nine minutes.

I started to do deep breathing techniques like they say to do for pain management when you're in labor.

In *two, three, four...* **out**, *two, three, four.*

I knew already that it was happening. It was just strange that it was finally happening in reality and not just in my fears. Ten minutes had passed and the doctor finally cleared his throat.

He talked in a very low, soft voice, "The problem with your baby's heart…." He began.

I sat still as I felt the impact of my biggest fear colliding with reality.

He continued to explain, but I heard nothing.

He pulled out charts. I saw nothing.

Colby reached over and grabbed my hand. *I felt nothing.*

All I could think of was how awful the doctor's voice sounded. *I can't **HEAR** YOU,* I just wanted to SCREAM at him. *Why are you talking SO QUIETLY? This is KIND OF important…. why aren't you **speaking CLEARLY**? WHAT are you SAYING?*

I got up from the table and walked out the door, dizzy. The hallway seemed narrow–too narrow–like it was suffocating me. I struggled to breathe through my panic. For some reason the lights were turned off, so I walked in darkness, opening up random doors to closets and patient rooms, trying to find the bathroom.

*Why are there NO LIGHTS **ANYWHERE**?* I felt the anger and frustration seething. At the end of the hallway I finally found a bathroom, locked the door and started weeping over the sink. I didn't know what any of it meant. Did a heart defect mean that she would die? What about her other organs? Could they function okay… if her **HEART** DIDN'T? I looked in the mirror at my face that was dripping with both hot tears and cold water and felt like I had seen this scene somewhere before. A dream? A fear? I wasn't sure; it was all just so strangely familiar.

Like it was all happening just like it was supposed to.

3

MERRY-GO-ROUND

"Beloved, do not be surprised at the fiery trial when it comes upon you to test you, as though something strange were happening to you. But rejoice insofar as you share Christ's sufferings, that you may also rejoice and be glad when his glory is revealed."

I Peter 4:12-13

Colby and I walked out the door into the bitter, Icelandic wind.

"I told you so." I sounded like a first grader.

"No," he shook his head. "You can't say that. You can't be afraid of EVERYTHING...ALWAYS say that something bad is going to happen, and then when ONE thing does go wrong, say that you were right." I felt annoyed that he was arguing, but bit my tongue before I could take any more of my emotions out on him. We were both in a state of shock, but instead of consoling each other, it felt like we were on opposing teams.

I stopped in mid step and pulled his arm so he would face me. "I just wanted you to stop, hug me and say, 'Wow, honey. *You were right.* **SO** RIGHT.'"

We parted ways to get our girls from their different schools, and I walked in a state of shock to get Darcy, our youngest. The wind made each step heavy and I buried my face deep in my scratchy, wool scarf.

I tried to process everything that had just occurred. *Our daughter is going to die,* I told myself. *And if she doesn't die, she will have serious problems for the rest of her life.* Looking back, I'm surprised that I was able to put one foot in front of the other and make the walk down the street, Grettisgata, to Darcy's daycare.

I began to reflect on what had happened in the doctor's office. It had been so strange. As I had sat numbly and watched Colby and the doctor talk, a Bible verse had come to my mind so loudly and clearly and perfectly that it confused me. I had never memorized it before or even thought about the verse before. Matthew 10:28: "Do not fear those who kill the body but are unable to kill the soul." I didn't know exactly what it meant or how it even applied to my situation, but strangely it had comforted me.

Also, right before we had left, the doctor had looked at me and given me a warning that was also strange. "Whatever you do, don't read about this on the internet."

I wondered what he meant by this advice. Would I find all sorts of horror stories that he wanted to protect me from? Why wouldn't he want me to know the reality of our situation? Although I didn't understand, I made a decision right there that I wouldn't so much as google *one* word of it.

I picked up my little three year old from school as the Icelandic sky began to change and threaten rain. She began to talk about her day and I hoped she didn't hear the lump in my throat as I tried to converse back.

We got home and sat our daughters down to tell them the news. Their eyes were so wide; *how could they sense something was wrong?*

"We went to the doctors today..." Colby started. "...and we found out that you are going to have a little sister."

"Yay..." their cheers were weak and light, as if the burden in the air made them hesitant to celebrate.

"The doctors also found out that something is wrong with your sister's heart. So, we need to pray for her..."

I don't know what else he said to them. All I could see were two confused little girls, nodding their heads with such brave grace. I turned my head so they couldn't see my eyes turning red and hot. *How sad,* I thought with annoyance and indignation. *Their celebration lasted about as long as mine.*

I tried to pack. We were scheduled to leave for Spain at 5:00 the next morning. It was our annual meeting with other missionaries from our region and, in an effort to enjoy some extra sunshine, we had added vacation days to the front end of the trip.

I didn't even want to go anymore.

I felt numb with shock as I threw flip-flops and swimsuits in the suitcase. I had no idea if we had everything we needed, but I didn't even care. I concentrated for a few minutes on packing, then quickly remembered that the baby in me had a mutated heart and felt my throat tighten.

I couldn't believe it was happening just like I had feared. I stopped what I was doing and stood still as a new thought struck me with impact: *Was it MY fault?* Was the heart defect a result of something *I had done?* Was it because of my recent trip to the Blue Lagoon, my diet that included pasteurized Danish cheese, or my pessimism?

The doctor had tried to assure me that it had nothing to do with my negligence, but did he really understand how thermal pools impact organ development? It was completely common for pregnant Icelanders to go to thermal pools, but maybe I shouldn't have followed suit. *If only I had been more careful...*It was hard to shut up the loud feelings down deep that told me **this was somehow my fault.**

My feelings slowly shifted from shock to anger. I went into the bathroom to pack contact solution, bitter that the joyful news of having another girl was robbed from us so quickly, as though I was entitled to and *deserved* such a glorious moment. All pregnancy long I had hesitated to celebrate. *What if I have another miscarriage? Don't get prematurely excited, Annie...Just wait until the ultrasound to celebrate.*

The room was blurry with tears and fears.

"What are you doing?" I asked as I looked over Colby's shoulder.

It had been a heavy evening as we had called both our parents on Skype to tell them the news of the ultrasound. I tried to decipher everyone's facial expressions as though they contained clues to whether or not our baby would survive. Colby's Dad looked down at the ground and shook his head ever so slightly; my mom gasped and covered her mouth with her hands as though **that** would hide her shock and concern.

Why is she so worried? Why is she so upset? Does she know something I don't? I analyzed everyone's reaction, grappling for someone to give me a sense of what to expect.

"Colby, are you done packing? What are you doing?" I attempted to sound curious and not critical (although it's most likely I was being critical).

Colby didn't answer, which meant that he was concentrating, so I leaned over, squinted my weary, burning eyes to read what he was writing about on our family blog.

www.getagarman.blogspot.com
March 29th, 2010

The Twenty-Week Ultrasound

I never knew that going to an ultrasound could be such a frightening experience until today. Nevertheless, I am thankful that technology allows us to prepare ourselves for the difficult time that appears to be ahead.

After the ultrasound technician was not satisfied with what she could see regarding the baby's heart, she suggested it might be good to have the doctor take a look. We moved to a new room and met the doctor as he began to study the baby's heart to see if there was any-thing to be concerned about.

Any explanation that begins, "The problem with your baby's heart…" is bound to put a lump in your throat, but we gathered our wits to be able to process the explanation that we received and I will try to summarize for you.

*Our little girl (yes it's a girl) has a heart defect. The initial diagnosis is that it is either **Critical Pulmonary Stenosis** (more likely) or **Pulmonary Atresia with Intact Ventricular Septum** (possibly). Either way it will require a procedure immediately after birth. Only time will tell whether the condition will be treatable with a catheterization or require a more extensive surgery. We will return to the doctor after our vacation and he hopes to be able to see better exactly what the situation is.*

If you have questions, we have few answers beyond the explanation above. It was unsettling and scary to hear and we have a lot to figure out leading up to the baby's birth in August. If you are reading this we desire that you would pray for the baby's health and for our peace of mind as we travel these next months with this burden on our hearts."

I had to laugh cynically. I had hoped to reveal the gender in a bit more dramatic fashion than just parentheses. I couldn't believe how much of the doctor's words Colby had retained.

The room had been spinning so fast, and it was as though I was in the corner puking while Colby was riding the same merry-go-round but with a calm, cool, and collected mind. *I didn't even know the name of the diagnosis until I read his words.*

It was funny. There wasn't the slightest temptation to read anything about it on the internet. There was a sense that...I guess...that it wouldn't change a single thing.

4

BREAKING BREAD

*"I have said these things to you, that in me you may
have peace. In the world you will have tribulation.
But take heart; I have overcome the world."*

John 16:33

The alarm went off at 4:25 AM and I almost dry-heaved as I sat up in bed. *Why are we still going on this trip,* I thought to myself as I scooted my ever-widening rear across the bed and tried to get down. The kids were tired and grumpy, I was shaky, and we loaded all our suitcases into our friend, Diana's car after eating a bowl of Icelandic Skyr.

On the drive to the airport, I thought of all the people I would be seeing in Spain. Everyone would innocently congratulate me and ask questions about my pregnancy, and I didn't want to talk about it at all. *I wasn't sure if the baby inside of me would survive, so I felt only **half-pregnant...like I was faking it or something**. I didn't want to pretend I was carrying life in me... it wasn't that simple.*

After boarding the plane, we started the journey south over the North Atlantic Ocean and I tucked my head deeply into the tray table in an effort to take a nap. After a few minutes I realized a nap wasn't going to be possible, but despite the uncomfortable strain the position was putting on my back, I felt like I was tucked in my Daddy's arms so I stayed there.

I tried to talk to God about my feelings.

I told Him that I wasn't mad at Him, just sad at Him. He could have prevented this with merely a word, but He didn't.

I pressed my head deeper and deeper into the tray table until it pinched my forehead and I imagined lowering myself deeper and deeper in submission to God's plan.

"Please, God…help me to not be angry at you. Please help me trust you. *I can't do that on my own.*"

※

Every step I took, every movement I made, I thought about the news. Customs. Baggage Claim. Taxi ride. While I poured drinks for my kids, took them on potty breaks, even chatted with other people, the whole time *I was having a second conversation with Jesus.* Mostly He was telling me that *it was okay,* and I was nodding inwardly. I thought of all the worst-case scenarios and He greeted each one with, *Even if that's the case, it will be okay.* The quiet conversation beneath all the other ones began to calm me…strengthen me…help me.

We checked in to our hotel and for a few moments the beauty of palm trees and warm air enveloped me. Despite the bad news I was carrying in my womb, I felt--for a moment--the grace of a world created by a good God.

The next morning, the sun was shining and we headed right for the beach. We ordered fried calamari at a restaurant that provided not only tables, but also--to our surprise--queen sized beds to lie on at the beach. Our children played in our shadows next to us in the sand while we sat together in the bed with a view of the Mediterranean Sea.

After an hour of napping to the sound of lapping waves and giggling children, I leaned over to Colby and told him I was ready to talk. He sat up immediately and gave me his full attention with such eagerness that I let out a confused laugh.

"Hey, when your wife's ready to talk, you better listen," he responded as he propped the pillows behind his back.

Even though I had *said* I was ready to talk, we sat still for a few moments as I thought about the ball of conflicting emotions in me. Eventually he broke the silence and asked me if I had been thinking about the news. I answered, "Yes. Every single moment."

"Me too." He said it quiet.

We both stared up at the blue and white marbled sky and then he began to ring out the wet towel of his thoughts. What came out was surprisingly mature and wise. I mean, sure, he was an ordained pastor, but this wasn't just a sermon. This was our lives.

In the bucket of his purged emotions, there was nothing but a strong trust that God had our best in mind, and whatever happened, God would see us through. He seemed shaken up on some level, but not afraid. *Cast down, but not destroyed....*

I just listened to him talk in the Spanish sun as he broke bread for my famished soul. Words that pointed me to the One who neither does wrong nor perverts justice. He made it sound so simple.

We talked until the sun started panting westward and our sun-kissed children started asking for something to eat. Only then did the conversation pause and turn to loading up beach bags and where we would eat dinner and if we would rent bicycles. Everyone carried something through the awkward sand as we headed to our hotel: the children with their towels, Colby with his bucket of trust, and me with my bucket not so sure and definitely not so pure.

❧

Ah, yes...*marriage.* It was something I claimed I would never participate in. Perhaps it was my desire to be the non-conformist at Liberty University and not leave with a ring on my finger. Perhaps it was my *pride* and my desire to always be chased and never be caught. Whatever the reason, I had made it clear to Colby that marriage wasn't for me.

The turning point came the summer of 2000. We parted ways for the summer, me to my home in Wisconsin and Colby to an internship with a church youth group in Florida. Like clock work, every Friday night he faithfully called my house in Wisconsin from his host home in Florida. Most Friday nights, I strategically left for the evening to avoid his call and see if he'd eventually give up. How much did he really like me? It was a cruel game but I wanted to see how far he would go to win my heart.

The game ended one Friday night when I called and found out the horrible news. Colby wasn't there; he was at a funeral.

A boy in the youth group had been run over by a trailer while they were at summer camp. I nearly dropped the phone as I felt my arms and legs go weak. My friend was going through something tragic and I had been busy stonewalling him. I wanted to run all the way to Florida and hug him and cry with him and be at his side as he went through something so terrible.

I knew at that moment I loved him.

I *would* say the rest is history, *but unfortunately I'm slightly more stubborn than that.*

After a full summer apart, we returned to Liberty University at about the same time. It was fun to each other again, and we sat on the mansion lawn as the sun set over the Blue Ridge Mountains, catching up on each other's lives. When the weekend arrived, Colby asked me if I wanted to go to the park together for a picnic.

My answer was a quick no. I lied and told him that I was booked solid all weekend. The truth was, my new roommate had simply *mentioned* that her parents were coming into town and she wanted me to meet them. Clearly I was skewed on how long this would take.

Colby didn't buy it. He kept digging until I admitted I had no real plans.

So it was that night, September 1st, 2000, that we drove to Riverside Park in Lynchburg, Virginia. As we stood above the James River in the thick humidity, he asked for a final time, "Has anything changed since the last time we've talked?"

I swallowed hard. It was as though there were two voices at war within me. One was a little girl that so desperately wanted to be taken care of and loved and adored, and another voice that screamed to the little girl, "Shut up! You don't need a man! You can do it on your own. Don't break down and admit weakness."

"Nothing has changed," I told him, but as the words were leaving my mouth I knew that I couldn't keep up the act for long. Something **had** changed. I loved him now and I didn't want to fight it any longer. Why was it so difficult to admit this?

Well, it turns out Colby couldn't take no for an answer *anyway.* "Why not?" he asked and I began to explain to him my unfulfilled desires to backpack Europe, hike Everest, and everything in between before entering into the "prison cell" of commitment. "So, you're looking for adventure in all the wrong places," was his simple response.

"God is the true adventure," he continued. "When you follow Him, He takes you to places that satisfy much deeper than anything you'd find on this earth." I knew this, but did I really? I could feel myself getting closer to the edge of something beautiful, yet unknown and terrifying.

We sat through a late afternoon rain shower. I continued to listen to him talk. Eventually the sun melted orange and purple over the horizon and I felt my heart do something similar. Twilight began to peek and we continued to talk as it spread across the sky. Around 11:30 pm, thirty minutes before our dorm's curfew, I finally said the words, "I really want to be with you." It was as though the small, honest voice had spoken for the first time. Neither of us knew what to say.

He waited for a "But..."

It never came.

Now, the edges of the unknown were right beneath my feet and it was terrifying yet irresistible. Colby grabbed my hand because he sensed the fear and dizziness of my soul teetering on the edge. "It's not like I'm asking you to get married or anything," he tried to reassure. "I'm not asking you to even have any kids…I'm just asking you to take one small step with me." Hand in hand, we took one step from where we were on the bench to the ground below.

"Okay," I agreed. One small step…even I could commit to that. He made it sound so easy.

I guess I should have known better.

One year later to the day, we stood at the altar and said, "I do" in the presence of our family and friends. And we lived happily ever after…well…*kind of…*

5

BATHROOM FLOOR

*"In this you rejoice, though now for a little while, if
necessary, you have been grieved by various trials,
so that the tested genuineness of your faith—more
precious than gold that perishes though it is tested by
fire—may be found to result in praise and glory and
honor at the revelation of Jesus Christ."*

I Peter 1:6-7

April 1, 2010
Malaga, Spain

On our second day in Spain, I found a book at the bottom of Colby's bag called "Counterfeit Gods." The title didn't strike me as something that would speak to me in my time of need, but I was desperate for anything to get my mind off my situation.

After the first chapter, I was hooked. God used the small book to profoundly speak to me and open my eyes to the many idols I was clinging to instead of looking to God to be my source of joy. It was surprisingly applicable to our situation and reading it was like putting on braces for my wobbly legs.

Every line I read, I turned into a prayer. Every page, a meditation. I bathed in each new thought and could feel lies washing away. The most surprising lie that I became aware of was that *I could only be happy if I got what I wanted.*

I could feel muscles being stretched and strengthened in places I didn't even know I had.

It hurt, but **it was a good hurt**. Like one that you know is making you stronger.

One evening, I rented a bike and went for a long ride on the boardwalk. As I passed many families, many children, and many *healthy* babies, I could feel the temptation to compare loud and strong. But, something strange and unexpected happened: God gave me the strength to not succumb to jealousy. Instead He gave me a new thought over and over, with each person I passed: **You don't know what their story is all about**.

With every block I rode, I decided to recount a way that God had blessed me. My own health, a faithful husband, two amazing kids, friends who would do anything for us, opportunities to travel...it was impossible **not** to feel lighter with every mile. *God gives me so much that I don't deserve,* I concluded. I felt a little stronger at the end of the ride as the stars started to come out.

Giving thanks...It felt like one baby step in the right direction.

Our organization's annual meeting in Malaga, Spain began on a Monday. Our meeting didn't start until the afternoon, so Colby took the kids to the Pablo Picasso Museum in town so I could rest. I lay in the hotel bed wishing I could fall asleep so that I didn't have to hear my thoughts so loudly.

I stared at the ceiling as the breeze blew the silk curtains in a rhythmic dance. Outside our room was the courtyard, and as people from our meeting began arriving I could hear their English voices ascending up through my window. I closed my eyes as I tried to bear up under the weight I could feel starting to descend. *The questions...there would be inevitable questions...*

That night after dinner was the first session and, after dropping our daughters off in the childcare room, we walked into a stucco room to recognize a few faces. The company we worked for had hundreds of missionaries in countries all over the world, but our meeting was only for the personnel serving in the Scandinavian cluster. It was a small group. Not easy to hide. Some we had met at training, some we had only seen through Skype, but most were total strangers.

We ended up in the front row and I scanned the room quickly to locate a bathroom if the need came up. The session started with prayer and then a blonde and blue-eyed couple came to the front to lead us in a time of worship.

The words came on the screen and I just watched as everyone in the room sang like normal people do at church. A lump started to burgeon in my throat and I could hardly swallow, let alone sing. *To God.*

It was the words. Something about the words. They spoke of God's goodness, His faithfulness...His protection. I had sung them before carelessly, but now I didn't know if I could sing them again. How could anyone?

A question began to emerge in the back of my heart, slowly and carefully like a baby spider emerging from its egg.

Was God good?

Yes, but was He *really*?

I looked around the room at everyone singing these words to Jesus and sneered inwardly. Did they really *know* what they were saying? Did they *really* believe this? Did they really know what could transpire in their lives *the next day* that could shake them to the very core? *Would they really be singing **this loudly** if they had a child with a possible death sentence in THEIR WOMBS?*

I didn't give permission for the tears to come, but they didn't ask and barged in anyway. My husband noticed and put his arm on my shoulder, but it didn't make it all better. The next song began but all I could think about was myself.

I wasn't in the mood to worship God. I had forgotten everything He had reminded me of the day before and *I didn't want to remember.* All I could see were people all around me who didn't have my problem, naïvely worshipping a God that I wasn't so sure I could trust to be good. It was hard to fight the negativity so I decided I wouldn't even try.

I was starting to cry now, and...let's be honest... it *wasn't pretty.* My back started to shake with every sob and I could feel copious amounts of saliva starting to drain from every opening on my face. As more and more attention was being drawn my way, I felt like I was trapped in a burning building with no exit strategy.

Even though the bathroom was at the very front of the room and I would have to walk right past the worship leaders, there was no choice. I left my seat and walked bravely in front of everyone to the bathroom where at least I could be safe with my own tears and saliva and convulsions. I locked myself in a stall and sat on the cold floor so that my heart would have a companion of the same temperature. I let myself cry for a long time, giving in to self-pity and anger and fear and confusion.

After awhile my husband knocked on the door, which was a strange situation since I wasn't sure whether or not I had the authority to let him in to the women's bathroom. He came in after not hearing a response and sat down uncomfortably on the floor next to me.

"Are you ready to go back now?" His eyes were pleading.

"Why do I have to go back?" I didn't care.

"Well, everyone saw you come into the bathroom...and it's a little strange if you never come back out." He was in pastor mode now.

I was not.

"I don't care what anyone thinks of me." I blew my nose loud and hard as if to make a point. "Besides, if I do come out everyone will see me and I don't want to make a scene." It was a totally inconsistent statement. "I don't want to be around anyone right now, okay? Why can't you get that?"

"*Annie...*" He sighed and closed his eyes as he realized that the next few hours of his life were going to be spent on the floor of a women's bathroom. He handed me another tissue without even looking my direction.

I'm not sure all that transpired in the following moments. I'm not sure what he said or what I said, all I remember is this deep pain of *feeling*. Was this how it felt for the shock to finally wear off? Everything I had ever believed was being tested and *surely I would fail the class*. The floor was hard, but my heart was harder and even that fact added to my anger.

I don't know how much time elapsed. The entire time I was mad at my husband who I felt was too concerned about *how our prolonged bathroom stay appeared to everyone in the conference room*. It was easy for me to judge; I had no one else I was thinking about other than myself.

I guess he couldn't have been as bad as I condemned him to be, because he sat with me and let me cry...no, wail actually...at a decibel level that surely everyone heard on the other side of the door. He prayed with me and for me and despite me. And, I don't know how he did it, but he somehow even managed to stand me up and wash my face and lead me out of the bathroom door to face an entire room staring in our direction.

We assumed our seats in the front row and he held my hand tight. I held on tighter, thinking loudly and clearly that *we all need someone to carry us out of the women's bathroom sometime*.

The first year of our marriage was exciting, like having a sleepover every night with your best friend. The week after our wedding, we moved to the suburbs of D.C. where the traffic was heavy and the mountains were far away. Colby was hired as the associate pastor at Stafford Baptist Church and I got a job teaching English as a Second Language (ESL) at an elementary school. We were in charge of a youth group, made new friends, and were learning just how bad we were at communication even though we had boasted about our skills at pre-marital counseling.

There were the normal conflicts like most married couples experience. Unfortunately, we were both passionate. And stubborn. And intense. And...well...*I think you get the picture.*

After a few years of youth ministry and working full time as an ESL teacher, I was completely burnt out. I didn't know how other teachers did it for so many years, and I didn't care to find out. I wanted a way out. It only seemed logical. Two of my friends had just done it and it seemed like the natural, next step.

The night the pregnancy test showed a double line, I dramatically fell onto the bathroom floor, knocking the ledge of the tub softly on my way down. Colby stood over me and I stared back at him with no answer to the question that he was wearing on his face.

I stayed on the floor a really long time, just looking at my stomach, trying to wrap my head around the fact that a live human being was inside of me. It had happened so quick; it was unfathomable.

The very first thing I did was go to my friend Jennifer's house (she had the *internet*) and google "how to prevent a miscarriage." This thing wasn't for sure yet so I didn't let myself get too attached to the idea. There was too much that could go wrong. At night, I dreamt that I gave birth to a pot roast with gray eyes. Other dreams included giving birth to a piglet and other strange creatures. I guess one could say I had *some anxiety* about the whole thing...

On October 17th, 2004 our little Haley Jane came into the world and completely turned it upside down. It was amazing to watch her mimic our facial expressions, smile, learn how to clap and crawl and dance and eventually run. Motherhood was more amazing than anything I'd ever experienced and I was thankful God didn't give me the life I thought I'd wanted. In fact, before long I was starting to have a desire to add another child to our family. This seemed border-line miraculous to both me and everyone who knew me...

I think Colby's old college roommate, Russ, said it best when He said, "The fact that Annie is married with a child *and wants another one* is proof that there is a living God."

It was time for lunch and our group walked down the open halls to the hotel cafeteria. Pastor Bill, our senior pastor, had brought a team of people from our home church, Stafford Baptist, to provide childcare for our meeting and we all hugged when we met. He had heard the news.

He sat next to us at lunch while we tried to get our girls to try Spanish olives and foreign cheese. Our girls were excited to see their old pastor and kept interrupting each other to tell him stories. "Whenever we stay up late, mom tells us that we're up PASSED our bedtime. One time I thought she said "PASSA bedtime," so now when we stay up, we call it PASSA BILL Bedtime!" They giggled and Darcy's curls bounced.

The conversation hadn't been going on for more than five minutes when Bill spoke up, "If you end up having to come back to the States, you can stay at our lake house."

Pastor Bill and his family owned a second home in Northern Virginia. I hadn't even thought of the possibility of going back to the States, so I'm sure the expression on my face was a little dumb-founded. But here he was, one step ahead, meeting a need that I didn't even realize existed.

Colby said thanks and I mumbled a thank you, not sure how it would all work out and not really wanting to think about it. There were so many unknowns and it felt like if I looked at them all long enough, they would swallow me whole.

The week went on and I did a lot of crying. Not a lot of talking, mostly hiding. I hated the feeling of my throat knotting when I had conversations, so I avoided them. Serious ones anyway. I let Colby do all the explaining. *Yes, we're having a baby in August. We just found out that our baby has a heart defect. We're not sure what's going to happen. There are a lot of details to work out.* I sat by his side like his mute wife as he explained and answered questions, still unable to comprehend that all of it was happening to *us* this time.

Our last day was bright and sunny and I had forgotten my sunglasses in the room. I sat outside with some women who lived and worked in Lithuania and I listened to their stories, trying to forget about mine. I closed my eyes in the sunshine and let it blind me.

Our final session came to an end, but before anyone could leave, one of the supervisors got out of her seat and came to the front to get everyone's attention.

"Before everyone leaves, we are going to have a surprise baby shower for Annie and Colby and their new little girl. Let's move our chairs in a circle. Everyone has brought some gifts from their countries to give to you."

It was a kind, but awful moment. Excited eyes turned to me and I numbly moved my chair so it was a part of the circle. Everyone was smiling, and I knew I should be too. This was, after all, my baby shower. *Baby showers are supposed to be happy.*

I opened up a gift bag labeled **Harrods** and slowly pulled out a beautiful stuffed bunny rabbit. "Every little baby deserves something from Harrods," the gift giver said. Everyone reacted with the expected *awwww* and cooed at the gift, but I just stared at it, unable to compete with the group's excitement. Would my baby ever see this? I started to **feel** again. Strongly.

Wonder.

Wrestle.

The whole room was waiting for my reaction.

What was happening? I felt sick as I picked up another gift from the pile. A swaddling blanket. I didn't even want to look at it. Would it ever be used? I didn't want to be unkind, but I could not muster any emotion to express my wobbly gratitude.

Booties from Estonia, a rattle from Lithuania, more stuffed animals from London. A swaddling blanket from Helsinki. I watched as my husband opened the rest, while thinking of how similar they looked to *pearls being cast before swine.* Someone prayed to close our time and I breathed a sigh of relief that the time had ended. These missionaries, these new friends… they were so kind and generous and loving…I just didn't know what to do with it all.

6

THIRD AISLE

*"Turn to me and be gracious to me, for I am lonely
and afflicted. The troubles of my heart are enlarged;
bring me out of my distresses."*

Psalm 25:16,17

We arrived back in Reykjavik just as the stars were appearing in the eastern sky on a calm night. Despite our jet lag and exhaustion, the next day came quickly. I rushed Haley and Darcy to Icelandic pre-school and arrived late as usual to Icelandic grammar class. Fortunate for me and my chronic tardiness, most of the class was also late and the whole atmosphere was rather laid back.

I nibbled on a croissant while we read a second grade level science book and talked about seasons of the year. Iceland didn't really have seasons like the ones illustrated in the book, and my mind drifted to my scenic hometown in Wisconsin. I brushed my finger over the picture of a child watering a tulip.

Would my children ever get to experience this as they grew up in Iceland?

Living in Reykjavik had, at times, been trying. Despite the beauty around me, I had definitely struggled with homesickness and culture shock. The hardest thing besides the spiritual darkness was the physical darkness. *And, the wind speed that nearly took my breath away.*

During break time, I lay down on a bench in the hallway, trying to reconcile the fact that I was no longer in seventy degree Mediterranean weather and would probably not feel the warmth of the sun for a few North Atlantic months. Colby sat beside me, one hand on my leg, the other holding his notebook so he could memorize new vocabulary words. Our teacher walked past and commented with a smile that I shouldn't be feeling so sick anymore since I was in my second trimester.

She wasn't trying to pry, but Colby took the opportunity to explain that the doctor had found something wrong with the baby. I didn't sit up or even give the courtesy of opening my eyes, but I could hear her stop and put her hand over her mouth. She was starting to cry and it made me, for some reason, horribly sad and mad.

"I'm so sorry," she didn't know what else to say.

Why was she crying? Had she heard of this heart defect before? Did she know that the baby would die? The heaviness was so great I felt as though I would never make it off the bench.

Somehow I did. Somehow I made it through class and somehow I had strength to carry my heavy backpack up the stairs and out the door. *Scratch that.* My husband most likely carried my backpack for me. It was time for another appointment. Colby went to get a cup of coffee and kissed me on the cheek, telling me he'd meet me at the clinic.

On my way to the clinic I stopped by the largest church in Iceland, Hallgrímskirkja, and got on my knees to pray deep in the third aisle so the tourists wouldn't get me in any of their pictures. *Lord, please give me strength.* My prayers had become increasingly brief. *I want to trust you no matter what happens, good or bad.*

At the cardiology center, the cardiologist did another fetal echo, which is an ultrasound of the baby's heart. He spoke and I understood his words despite his accent and soft voice that really wasn't bad at all, I now realized.

I stared at him while he explained our baby's condition, my thoughts wandering as I imagined the stress he must face in his job, wondering **what grounds him** in this unstable world. I prayed for him while I listened. That he would find a center as the world spun like a merry-go-round around him. That I would trust The Center that I knew to be true.

Critical Pulmonary Stenosis. I wrote that new vocabulary word down in my journal. I'm sure he had said it last time, but this time I was able to hear it. If this turned out to be her condition, there was a possibility that she would just need a small procedure called a catheterization. He wasn't sure, though, and there were lots of possibilities of what could happen.

They didn't do pediatric operations like this in Iceland, so we would need to fly to the States, possibly Boston Children's Hospital. *How long before she would recover?* I had so many questions this time and I was feeling the clouds part in my head, making way for some clarity.

If she had Pulmonary Stenosis, it was a possibility that recovery would only be a few days. He told us the range of possibilities, but reminded us that we wouldn't know for sure until
she was born.

I looked at my husband and felt myself begin to think
clearer. There was a range of things that now I could expect,
but we would just have to wait and see.

I walked to get Darcy, our youngest, from school, stopping
first at Hallgrímskirkja to return to my knees for a prayer of
thanksgiving. Perhaps her condition would be mild and only
need a small procedure. I felt lighter as I considered this possibility...*and tried not to think of what would happen if her condition
ended up being worse.*

I opened up my computer after Icelandic class to take a quick
break and read something in my mother tongue to soothe my
aching head. We had been studying Icelandic since we had
arrived in Iceland in 2009 and it was an absolute marathon.
Despite many tears (and many days I thought I was fighting
off a virus *but I was actually just mentally exhausted*), I was finally
starting to get the language.

Each week I met with Thora, a university student, who
let me practice my embarrassing three-year-old level language skills and encouraged me as I toddled along. The
Icelandic kid's show, Lati Baer (Lazy Town) was a helpful
tool and we would watch it together, pressing pause every
thirty seconds as I wrote new vocabulary words down in my
notebook.

Not only was learning the language helpful in and of itself, but it also opened up new pathways to discovering Icelandic culture. Nearly all of the people on the small Island of approximately 300,000 people were members of the Icelandic State Lutheran church, but most I would venture to say, weren't convinced that the God of the Bible even existed.

Some Icelanders believed in elves that inhabited local hills that were also known as "hidden folk," but most weren't convinced of Jesus who claimed to be God in the flesh. Lutheranism was really a thin veneer covering their agnosticism. Since living there, my own faith had gone through somewhat of a crisis as I was forced to question everything I had ever been handed as true.

As I scrolled through my usual spots in cyberspace I noticed that our blog had been updated by my husband. I grabbed a pear to nibble on, put my feet up on the coffee table, and started to read what he had to say.

www.getagarman.blogspot.com
April 14th, 2010

Ultrasound Remix

We returned to the doctor on Monday for another ultrasound in hopes of gaining a little more information about the baby's heart condition. After some time, the doctor spent some time explaining his findings and answering our questions. We are really appreciative of the medical staff at Barnaspitali here in Reykjavik for spotting the problem and helping us get started on the journey. So here is what we learned on Monday...

1. *The doctor is pretty confident that it is Critical Pulmonary Stenosis rather than Pulmonary Atresia with Intact Ventricular Septum*
2. *There is a good possibility that a Catheterization may be able to take care of the problem*
3. *The Pulmonary Artery looks good and he thinks there may be some blood getting through to it. If so, it means there may be at least a small needle opening in the valve.*

Over the past few weeks we have had the opportunity to settle into the reality of the situation and come to a better understanding of it. As a result, some of the fears have subsided. We rest in God's grace that has been evident in ways that I hope to be able to explain at a later time.

*Without waxing too theological, we are thankful for the confidence we have in **God's love for us** in the midst of difficulty. We have always believed that God's purposes in the world are more complex, interesting, and mysterious than simply providing us with individual safety and comfort.*

*Many of the events in life help us to understand where our greatest GOOD and most certain JOY can be found, as well as where it cannot be found. It **cannot** be found—though we often look for it—in our own health and vitality — for they are merely*

*gifts when we possess them, meant to **point us to
their giver.***

*We believe that **God Himself** is our greatest good and
deepest joy and trust that through this experience he will
give us a greater measure of Himself to know and enjoy
by faith. The **hope** that we have through Christ making
a relationship to God available to us is the same hope
that the Apostle Paul writes about when he reminds us
that "nothing can separate us from the love of God that
is found in Christ." (Romans 8:38-39). That "**nothing**" includes the fears that accompany finding out that
your baby will be born with a heart defect.*

*And for **that** we are grateful.*

I finished reading my husband's blog post and sat back on the
uncomfortable wing back chair in our furnished apartment.
Out the huge windows that nearly reached our ceiling was the
sherbet sunset that seemed to linger for hours.

I wasn't sure how I felt about the pronoun "we."

Sure, he was trying to include me in his assessment of how
we were doing, but it really wasn't an entirely accurate picture of my heart. Coping with the reality? Yes. Thankful?
Hmmm...*not so much.*

Colby sounded so solid...so confident in God's purposes
being worked out for the ultimate good...so spiritually mature. I felt like my stability was more circumstantial. When I
reflected on how minor her condition could end up being, I

felt fine. If my thoughts wandered to how things could easily turn, I didn't feel so strong. I wondered how I would react if we found out it was worse. Could I really take it? Could God really be trusted? I knew the answer in my head, *but my heart still needed to learn...*

7

EYJAFJALLAJÖKULL

"And those who know your name put their trust in you, for you, O Lord, have not forsaken those who seek you."

Psalms 9:10

The days in April passed rather quickly. I distracted myself from thinking about the serious things happening inside of me by reading Icelandic short stories and conjugating Icelandic nouns. Although it had tried, Icelandic had not defeated me, and I was feeling the sense of accomplishment that comes from conquering something very difficult. (Okay, maybe *conquering* is too strong a word…). All the Icelanders we met appreciated that we were learning their language and it opened doors to new conversations.

Although I knew we would have to fly back to America for the baby's cardiac procedure, it sounded like we would possibly return to Iceland shortly and reap the benefits of all our hard work in the language. It had taken a long time, but

Iceland was beginning to feel like home. It was becoming impossible to go for a walk through the city center of Reykjavik and not run into someone we knew. To me, that was the definition of finally being settled.

I loved the colorful rooftops in the otherwise monochromatic city of Reykjavik, the quaint cobblestone streets of downtown, and the mountains that provided a striking backdrop to the landscape. Outdoor thermal pools (think: Olympic-size hot tubs) dotted every single neighborhood and the kids were in childhood heaven every time we went.

The country was unique and deeply textured with art, history, and free-spirited people. The only thing that I didn't love was the biting Icelandic wind.

As we continued living life in Reykjavik, most of our friends and acquaintances became aware of our baby's heart defect. Everyone we shared with was noticeably saddened by the news, and after awhile I noticed a pattern: *most people had no idea what to say to comfort me.*

Some people said they were sorry. Some people asked a lot of questions. Some people, however, told me to "**Just have faith.**" This was the most confusing comment of all. What did they mean? *Just have faith that God would heal her? Just have faith that she would live?* This was difficult to deal with on multiple levels. How were they confident that God would do these things? And, did God's decision to heal her *depend entirely on my faith?*

On a rainy day in mid-April, I was getting ready for class when I heard Colby in the other room.

"Woah…"

I stopped what I was doing and came quicker than usual to the place he was sitting.

Images of a massive volcano filled the TV screen. Smoke, lightening, ash, floods, and fire…my husband commented on every detail from behind where I stood. What was going on? *Where was this happening?*

"They've been waiting for this one to erupt for years; It's only like eighty miles away from us," he explained as we both stood watching the live footage.

I didn't like it. It was only beautiful in an exotic kind of way. It was only beautiful if it was at a safe distance. I wasn't convinced it was.

"We've got to rent a car and go see it," he said.

I didn't respond.

Haley and Darcy came in and Colby excitedly showed them the natural, glorious disaster. They swooned over the images they were seeing and asked tons of questions, as I stood watching, rather unsure.

Ash--tons of ash--from the volcano was being catapulted all the way across the Atlantic Ocean. Not just flights, but **entire airports** all across Northern Europe were being shut down because of this one small volcano with a big name that no one seemed to be able to pronounce.

This volcano seemed to be a significant thing and I began to get nervous the longer I watched. I looked down, quietly put my hand on my belly, and wondered about all the implications.

Looking back, it really was a miracle of God that I wanted another child after Haley Jane. Little Darcy Elaine entered our world in May of 2006. She was a good baby and *it was a good thing*. Nearly every night following her birth, intense hot flashes would wake me up out of a dead sleep. Nothing, not even cold rags or a cold basement relieved the heat. At the ripe age of twenty-five, I was found commiserating with all the menopausal women at church.

Hormonal imbalance. Insomnia. Anxiety attacks. I wasn't sure how other mothers kept it together so well and concluded that I just wasn't as good. Sweet Darcy just slept the year away, oblivious to how her departure from my body had wreaked havoc on it.

It was during this particular low season of my life that our church decided to start a work in Iceland. I think it all began when Pastor Bill watched a documentary about this tiny island in the North Atlantic. He had wanted to take a missions trip to Reykjavik, but there were no Southern Baptist missionaries there at the time. Our pastors then became convinced that God was calling our church to help spread the gospel there with our resources.

Each of the pastors at Stafford Baptist decided to go with their families to Iceland for three months. In January of 2007, our little family (Haley was two, Darcy was seven months) left for Reykjavik and spent three months there, meeting people and seeing where and how God was working.

It was an incredible experience that in many ways felt like a long, cold vacation. Every day that went by, I felt my body starting to recover. Haley was obsessed with the church bells that rang from Hallgrímskirja, Darcy was a happy baby who loved the thermal pools, and we all loved exploring a new place. We came back home to Virginia three months later with many pictures to share and stories to tell.

But something didn't feel right.

My dear friend Charity was getting married that next summer and I flew to California to be in her wedding. Before I left, I had grabbed "To the Golden Shore," a biography on Adoniram Judson. *Surely I didn't know what I was getting into.* Adoniram had been a missionary to Burma in the early nineteenth century and the book recorded his adventures in following Christ oversees.

As I read his story on the flight, I became overwhelmed with emotion. As a child, I had dreamed of spending my life on the mission field, sharing the love and message of Jesus. As a teenager, I had gone on various mission trips with my youth group and had even gone on a few as an adult. Mission work had always been something I was passionate about, but the opportunity to go full-time had never been presented.

Until now.

We had returned from our short-term trip thinking that our time in Iceland was over. But now, alone in my window seat 50,000 feet above the ground, I began to wonder...

Was God calling us to return to Iceland full-time? It only seemed logical. Soon our kids would be getting older and there would be many excuses for why we couldn't go and serve overseas. There was a window of time and we needed to seize it.

As we flew over Wyoming, I fiercely journaled all sorts of questions. *God, it is SO expensive there...how will we afford healthy food? Afford clothes? How will we school our children? Ever have a date night? It is so cold and dark…how can I raise a family in such an environment? What about…*

I hadn't even talked to my husband yet.

I returned a week later and waited until the kids were asleep to sit down and tell Colby how God had been working in my heart.

There was only one problem. I couldn't stop crying.

Repeatedly, I started to open my mouth, but could not find the words or the courage to speak.

Once the words left my mouth, I **knew** that wheels would turn and move… and life as I knew it would never be the same. Colby had a heart for the mission field like I did. I knew that any interest on my part would result in him taking it seriously and somehow this would really happen.

After many, many minutes of unsuccessfully trying to speak, my baffled and concerned husband interrupted.

"Just tell me…It's okay…." His eyes were blue and worried.

I looked back into his eyes, so afraid to speak and change the course of our future.

"Annie…just tell me…

"I'm trying…" was all I could muster up.

Eventually, after guessing various scenarios about why I couldn't stop crying (One to which I responded, *"Are you serious? Who do you think I am?!"*), I finally told him that I thought we should return to Iceland as long-term missionaries. He responded by saying, "That's exactly what I've been thinking too."

I let out a dramatic sigh of relief.

Apparently God had been speaking loud enough for both of us to hear.

That week we began the process of applying as missionaries through the International Mission Board (the Mission Board of the Southern Baptist Convention). We would resign the following year and begin the process of moving our family to the northern-most capital of the world.

8

IMAGINATION

*"I call upon you, for you will answer me, O God;
incline Your ear to me; hear my words. Wondrously
show your steadfast love, O Savior of those who seek
refuge."*

Psalm 17:6

April 2010

It was a late-April evening, and on this particular night
another volcano erupted, only this time, it was inside our
apartment...

"It just feels like the most important decision of our entire
lives...like everything hangs on what we decide..." I buried my
face in my knees, unable to compete with the gravity of the
situation.

Colby's eyes were round and focused as he stared at the
computer screen.

We had just received an email from the mission board with rather unexpected news: I had to return to the States *immediately*. It was not recommended for me to fly in my third trimester and they wanted me on the other side of the ocean as soon as possible to see an American cardiologist and finish my pregnancy.

I had one week left of Icelandic classes, which meant I was reading Icelandic short stories, writing papers and preparing to take tests. It felt like I'd been going a hundred miles an hour in one direction...only to find out it was the wrong direction. It didn't matter if I passed the verb tense quiz...*it was time to move across the ocean...*

I gnawed on the tip of my finger as I waited for Colby to finish reading the email. This news was forcing to us to make a huge decision: where to we deliver the baby and have the cardiac procedure done. And where to **live** in the meantime.

The decision had to be made *soon*.

"Well, what's the best hospital that treats this kind of heart defect?" was the logical next step. I voiced it out loud even though it was obvious Colby was already thinking of it.

I sat in an uncomfortable position next to Colby, trying to see the computer as he googled "best pediatric cardiac hospitals in the USA." He scrolled through the 2009 US News and World Report and I gave myself the best backrub I could muster up. The fifty best hospitals for pediatric cardiology and heart surgery started with Boston. Then Texas Children's. Philadelphia. Children's Healthcare of Atlanta...

I looked at each option, petrified that we would choose the wrong one and put our daughter's life in jeopardy. How could we possibly know which surgeon's hands were the most stable? How could we determine which nurses were the most equipped?

The decision felt weighty. Like so much of it depended on us.

The room was starting to feel red hot as we argued about which option was best for us. We had almost four months until the baby's due date. Where would we live in the meantime? Ronald McDonald houses were a good resource, but we would only be able to get on a waiting list once the baby arrived. Pastor Bill had offered us his home, but I didn't know if we should take him up on his offer. At the same time, we didn't want to ask our family to put us up for that long.

I wasn't sure how it was all going to work out and it was a logistical nightmare.

There were so many factors to consider, and we couldn't seem to agree on anything.

It was as though God had put us in my mother's old pressure cooker from the 70's and it was whistling as the top rattled out of control. These decisions felt life shaping; how could we make them so quickly? The stress was building up like a restless volcano, which was *ironic* of course because of what was happening just outside our apartment. *I just hoped our ash trajectory wasn't as destructive.*

For the next several days, I woke up every morning and looked out the window to see if the wind had changed directions and the ash had come to Reykjavik. Night after night, the volcano made worldwide headlines as airports all over Northern and

Western Europe were shut down. *"We asked for cash...NOT ASH"*was the catchphrase that started circulating around the internet.

My stomach tightened with every news report. Iceland didn't have the resources to treat pediatric cardiac patients. How long would this volcano endure? How long would European flights be grounded? Night after night I laid in bed wondering how long it would take to travel by boat to America and if it would really come to that.

We scheduled flights to New York City for the kids and I for early May. Selling Haley and Darcy on the idea of going back to the States wasn't hard at all. Colby's parents would pick us up from the airport and we would stay with them a little while. Eventually they would drive us down to northern Virginia where we used to live. We convinced our kids that it was all one big glorious adventure, which--of course--it was.

It had taken some time, but we eventually decided to take Pastor Bill up on his offer, live at their house in Virginia and have Gracie at UVA Children's Hospital in Charlottesville, Virginia. Since we would be living an hour and a half away from the hospital, getting to appointments would be simple and easy on the whole family.

Colby got a flight to arrive in Virginia at the end of May. Our company would give us a stipend for food and gas and keep us on their insurance until after the birth when they would determine the next step. If all went well, we would return to Iceland within a month of the birth. If it didn't... well...then things could get a little tricky.

The day we left, we kissed Colby goodbye at the terminal and Darcy kicked and screamed as she left her father at the gate. I drug her onto the airplane and thought empathetically, for the first time really, of all the single mothers out there who felt like this every single day. The entire flight I prayed that the ash wouldn't somehow get in the engines and take us down.

The next day, the wind changed direction, the ash came, and the airport in Iceland was closed.

$\mathcal{Q}$

Blog post
www.getagarman.blogspot.com
May 9th, 2010

Coming Home

Last Thursday the girls and I headed to the airport in Iceland and said goodbye to Colby. He'll be joining us in 3 weeks after he finishes up some stuff in Reykjavik.

Darcy was very angry and defiant after he kissed us goodbye, and it was obvious that she was just scared about the whole transition (especially without Daddy). I felt like I was a single mother as I dragged her to our gate, reflecting on how quickly our plans had changed in just one short month.

*This was the kids' **22nd flight** just in the last 14 months, so they knew the drill. They watched Angelina the Ballerina for the entire five-hour flight and didn't make a sound.*

During our descent into JFK airport in New York City, I started to get really hot, dizzy, nauseous, dehydrated and weak. It was difficult to breathe and I knew I needed to do something immediately. The flight attendants were all buckled in their seats in the back waiting to land, so I did the only thing I knew to do: I stood up as much as I could with a seatbelt on and shouted, "I REALLY need some water. RIGHT. NOW."

Water bottles started flying toward and I literally opened them up and poured them all over my head and body. I tried to breathe slowly through my nose and control my breathing. We landed and I was still so sick I thought I would need a wheelchair to get through customs and baggage.

I waited until everyone exited the plane and three women (one a nurse) helped me get the kids and all our stuff off the plane. Long story short, after eating a whole package of Fruity Mentos, I didn't need the assistance cart that was called and I managed to get our seven bags and car seat through customs by myself where Colby's Dad was waiting for me. (He later told me he didn't recognize me because my hair was all wet).

Haley (who was pushing Darcy in the stroller that was also loaded down with stuff), got so excited when she saw her Pappy that she ran toward him and tripped, making Darcy and her stroller fall backwards. Needless to say, we made quite the entrance.

Last night we drove through the night and through the mountains to Colby's quaint hometown of Galeton, Pennsylvania. Darcy threw up and I felt so sick and uncomfortable I just wanted to camp out on the side of the road. We'll be heading to Pastor Bill's lake house in Virginia soon…

As for today, I celebrated my return to the States by eating marshmallow fluff, Fig Newtons, Frosted Flakes, and Combos.

God Bless the USA.

It was my first morning in America and despite the jet lag and exhaustion, excitement of familiar soil woke me up early. The phone rang and it was Colby in Iceland. As I started to answer the phone, I stepped out onto the front porch in my pajamas and felt the morning sun on my face. The air was warmer than any day I had experienced in Iceland and I could feel energy rising as the rays sunk in deep. I couldn't get over how many American flags there were, proudly displayed on seemingly every house on the street.

"So…what do you think?" were his first words.

"A-MER-ica! A-MER-ica! God shed his grace on Thee!" I sang in response.

He made a sound that was a cross between a groan and a laugh.

"And crown Thy Good with—"

"Okay, okay, I get the picture, " he cut me off, clearly embarrassed from the other side of the ocean as though his old neighbors could see *him* too.

Colby's parents would soon be taking us to Virginia. They would stay for a couple of days to help while I had my first pediatric cardiology appointment. I would hardly be alone. My parents made a sporadic decision to fly to Virginia and see us, so they would be with us the remainder of the time before Colby arrived. It was strange, but the spring sunshine in combination with seeing family made the trial almost feel like a blessing.

Almost.

If you used your imagination.

9

BACKSTORY

*"But my eyes are toward you, O God, my Lord; in
you I seek refuge; leave me not defenseless."*

Psalm 141:8

2008

When we told little three-year Haley that we were moving to Iceland, she only had one question. "Can I go with you?" We hugged her, relieved that her only concern was so easily taken care of.

After a nine-week training, we were ready to start our new lives in Iceland. There was only one slight problem. Our visas had not yet arrived.

We had left a stable job and rented our home out, yet did not have permission to live in the country we had sacrificed so much to go to.

What does one do? I'm not sure, but *we* drove to my sister in law's house in Pennsylvania and asked if we could stay there for a couple of weeks while we waited for the visas (that surely would *come any day*). Colby's sister, Brooke, was so generous and said yes, but the poor thing did **not** know what she was agreeing to.

One day as we were sitting on Brooke's couch watching the evening news, scenes of riots and picketing filled the screen. Nothing in particular captured my attention until I heard the words *Iceland* and *bankrupt* and *national financial crisis.*

The country's major banks failed and were taken over by the government. The economy in Iceland had crashed and the people were irate. We watched as rioters threw things at the parliament building and envisioned our little, lonely pile of visa applications sitting in a forgotten pile on someone's desk inside. Iceland's economy was a topic of international interest, and we weren't sure where we fit in to all of it.

Little Haley slept in Brooke's walk in closet and our little Darcy was in a pack and play in Brooke's bedroom. We passed the days by visiting family and touring Lancaster County. Colby's brother also lived there, so it was like one long family reunion. Colby's parents came down from Northern Pennsylvania to see us, my parents flew from Wisconsin to see us, and it was like one big party. *For the first month.* Eventually it began to feel more like an awkward vacation that didn't know when to end.

Finally, on December 15th, the much-anticipated day arrived and Colby received an email from the Icelandic Government. I was in the basement with the kids and I heard Colby upstairs yelling down to me that he got an email. I rushed upstairs where my other sister-in-law, Jen, was and heard Colby reading the email out loud to her.

DENIED. Our Visas had been denied.

I know I screamed and held my hands over my mouth for a good five minutes before I was able to speak or think. We all just stood there looking at each other watching the future that we had imagined disintegrate. Colby, ever the level headed one, tried to assure us that it would be fine. We could reapply for the visas and surely they would be granted. We could all proceed normally as though nothing happened at all.

After the initial shock wore off, it was time to tell everyone the news. Everyone's reactions made us question so many things. *Would the visas just be denied again?* Would we have to look for another job and find another place to live? How long could we live in such a state of uncertainty?

Nearly two more months went by, we did everything a tourist could do in Lancaster County, ate more ham than we had in the past decade, *and went and visited people we had already said goodbye to.* It was like one long, never ending goodbye. Before we decided to completely change plans and move on to something else, we consulted with our supervisor at the mission board and made a decision. We would go to Iceland on our passports.

Even though it meant the same amount of uncertainty and still waiting for the visas, in February of 2009 we got on an airplane and headed to Reykjavik...

Living in Reykjavik, Iceland without visas was like going to Disney World without being allowed to ride any rides. Our kids weren't allowed to enroll in pre-school. We couldn't enroll in the state language programs. We couldn't get a library card. We couldn't even rent movies, for Pete's sake. Life was hard feeling like an outsider and this only made matters worse.

Every single day we checked our email, but were consistently met with silence.

To busy ourselves and feel somewhat productive, we found a private Icelandic school to take Icelandic classes at. When we first walked in to "Iceschool," we were surprised to see that the classroom also doubled as the teacher's junk room. An old sink, a broken toilet, along with various other treasures lined the back of the room. Colby and I weren't sure whether or not to stay, but after getting to know the only other student (a nice guy from Greenland) and meeting the teacher (a large, jovial man who wore a Hawaiian shirt every day), we knew we had stumbled upon something special. Going to Iceschool gave us the structure and routine we needed to survive an ambivalent time.

Three months came and went and the visas had still not been granted. It was hard to know what to do. Would anyone know or even care if we stayed? Eventually we concluded that, *although the laws were ambiguous*, we needed to exit the "Shengen Area" of Europe.

My response to our exit from Iceland was *excitement*. "It's like we're riding a crazy rollercoaster...so, let's put our arms up and enjoy it!" Colby's response was a little less thrilling. "Yeah...well, I'm puking over the side of the rollercoaster."

Since England was outside the Shengen area and there were other missionaries living there, we decided that was our next destination. It was like a weeklong field trip. We toured castles, visited London, went on picnics, but lingering over all of it like a drizzly cloud was the ambiguity of our lives. After

ten days, we returned to Iceland for another three month period on our passports, knowing that if the visas didn't come in
the next 90 days we would have *to leave Iceland for good.*

The tension was high. The stress of uncertainty was heavy
to wear, especially over the cloak of culture shock. There was
so much heaviness and exhaustion, but right before I felt we
would snap in half, God would do something to relieve the
stress and lift the heaviness so it was bearable.

Fast forward to July...I had just had a miscarriage while
camping in the Northern part of the country; our renters had
caught our Virginia townhome on fire and it needed to be
completely renovated; A friend had just died from a roadside
bomb in Afghanistan. We were in low spirits and to top it off,
"Icelandic Summer" was an absolute joke. It snowed in June and
I was growing as numb as the wind. The visas were looking
more and more elusive every day.

The three-month period on our passport was quickly coming to an end. It appeared that our dream of planting a repro-
ducible, gospel-centered church in Reykjavik was never going
to be realized. Our mission board was sending us to Finland
where we would stay the rest of the year unless by some miracle the visas came. I can remember packing for Finland praying that at the very least, I would feel the sunshine warming
my skin there.

Jyvaskyla, Finland was an amazing respite and I started to
pray that the visas would never come. The Scandinavian summer lingered long and I spent as much time outside as I could
soaking in its last rays. One particular day, a man actually
came out of his apartment to check on me (I was lying down,
sunbathing in a patch of grass next to the parking lot after I
took the trash out...*apparently that was not normal behavior*). We

lived on a street (pronounced Poopoohoota) in a furnished apartment and rode the city bus everywhere we needed to go.

Finland was a time of searching and trusting and growing and listening. Would we ever get the visas? What would happen to us if we didn't? Had we made a bad decision uprooting our lives to try to spread the message of Jesus in Iceland? What *exactly* was God doing to us?

September 9th, 2009
It was a gorgeous late summer day and we were enjoying it at the home of our new Finnish friend, Irma. Irma owned a lovely piece of property in the outskirts of town and had invited our family and our friends over for the day. We had just sat down for afternoon coffee when Darcy busted in the front door screaming, "*I have to go to the baf-room!*" Colby got up to help her when I heard his phone ring. My stomach immediately dropped and the Finnish fancy cake I was chewing on suddenly felt heavy.

This was it. It had to be. We had been waiting for thirteen months and nine days to get a visa and it was the day we were told we would hear the decision. I made eye contact with my friend knowing that something life-altering was happening in the other room.

I excused myself and entered the bathroom where Darcy was loudly trying to get Colby's attention because she needed to be wiped, and Colby was *hiding in the shower with one hand plugging his ear,* trying to hear the person on the other end of the phone. He was smiling with a giddiness that I hadn't seen in a long time, and I leaned into the phone just in time to hear the words, "**You have been approved**." It was almost visible—the weight that I watched lift from Colby's shoulders...the burden that had been there for so long that I had begun to not even recognize it.

He continued to talk on the phone with our representative from Iceland, and I made my way to the closest chair in sight and collapsed in it. I watched him pace back and forth around the living room, laughing, glowing. We made eye contact. He moved the phone away from his lips and mouthed to me, "**It. is. over.**"

I couldn't believe it. I sat in the rocking chair in a state of shock for a long time. I don't know if anyone ever wiped Darcy. Colby was laughing and spinning the girls around in circles. Everyone was laughing, but I couldn't stop crying. All I could hear were the words, "*It is over.*" All I could see in my mind was a long and painful road that we had finally--hand in hand--come to the end of. Not just us, but many that had traveled this road with us were behind us cheering and smiling. I didn't know what to think. For so long we hadn't known WHEN this would end, WHERE it would end or if it WOULD ever end. And now it was over. The journey was **finally** over. *And it was finally beginning...*

10

WATERFALLS

"I cry to you, O LORD…Attend to my cry, for I am brought very low."

Psalm 142:5

May 17ᵗʰ, 2010
Locust Grove, Virginia

I awoke my first day back in Virginia to the sound of rain tapping and the ground drinking. Had I not had any responsibilities, I would have gone back to bed, letting the rain sing me a soft lullaby. But the kids were hungry. And I needed to find internet access and directions to University of Virginia's Pediatric Cardiology Ward because the big appointment was at 1:00. And I had to stop shaking long enough to think clearly.

I rolled off the bed and onto my knees, my stomach brushing lightly on the Berber carpet.

"God, I need strength to hear the news. Even if it's worse."

I stayed still for a long time, listening to the muffled sound of my kids trying to reach into a cereal box, trying to get my heart rate to slow.

"I think it's going to be worse." I scratched those words into my journal.

My sweet mother-in-law, Connie, rode with me to the appointment and held the directions tight as we drove Route 20. The road twisted and curved like the crooked vines climbing the trees outside our windows. Like the steering wheel I clutched. And a little bit like our lives.

We parked and walked through the rain to the hospital. I didn't even wear a coat. After the Icelandic winds, the warm rains felt inviting and hospitable.

We nibbled on turkey sandwiches and I wished I had packed more food even though it was hard to swallow the food I had. We sat in the waiting room and I distracted myself by cleaning out the cards in my wallet. I took out my driver's license and noticed that it would expire the next day. *I could relate.*

We met the cardiology team and they were all very kind, but no one talked during the ultrasound of the heart. I didn't understand everything I was seeing on the screen, but I assumed the red represented the blood. I squinted. It looked as though blood was not circulating throughout every chamber of the heart. I wasn't sure. I decided to close my eyes, relax the muscles in my neck, and pretend the dark, quiet room was a spa.

It lasted over thirty minutes. The fetal echocardiogram. The pictures of the valves and arteries. The scary silence as the cardiologist worked like an archeologist uncovering our future.

The lights came back on. I sat up, embarrassed while a room full of doctors watched me wake up. The main pediatric cardiologist, Dr. Dan, rolled his chair to my side and spoke with a soft voice. He had had this conversation before. You could tell. But this time, it was with me. And this time it was my life...and did he really care as much as his eyes said he did?

"Her...*is it a her?*...Her pulmonary artery and tricuspid valve are significantly blocked. Because the artery is closed, the right side of her heart is not developing."

He had charts showing the heart's anatomy, but they were all in black and white and I had absolutely no idea what I was looking at. I nodded to be polite as I listened to the words that seemed to swirl in the air. *Stenosis...Flow equals grow...if the blood doesn't flow, then the artery can't grow...*

He stopped.

"Do you want me to slow down? I know this is a lot..."

I just stared at his chart and smiled weakly at his kind request. I didn't know if there was anything he could do to get me to understand. I couldn't think. I could only feel.

Feel the ground rumbling. Feel the rug being pulled. Feel the instability shaking. Feel the chandeliers swinging. Feel the future being uncovered.

He began to speak again. "We can't know for sure...but this appears to be very serious. Your baby will most likely need an **open-heart surgery** immediately after she's born. And then another one five months later. She will need a total of three surgeries in three years."

There it was.

I can remember it vividly. The whole room filled with Doctors and students and fellows and nurses and residents watched me for a silent, suspended moment. I took a long and deep breathe and pretended to be brave. I couldn't cry. Not with everyone watching me. I just said *Okay.*

A very soft *okay.* It will be okay. They all seemed to believe me.

And I seemed to believe them believing me.

The phone rang, but I didn't want to answer it. I was light-headed as I drove us back home on the same curvy roads that only seemed to be getting curvier.

Unknown caller.

It had to be Colby calling from Iceland. Wanting to know what the pediatric archeologist had discovered.

"Do you want me to answer it?" Connie asked. Such a perfect mother-in-law. Never imposing, never controlling... *always just wanting to help.* I didn't, but I knew his butterflies were still banging wild and he deserved to know.

She answered the phone so I could maneuver the turns.

"Yes. Um...yes."

Her answers were short and she didn't know how much to say.

It was quiet for a moment, and then she tipped the phone away from her mouth to ask me a question. "He wants to know what the doctor said today."

She tried her best to explain.

We all sat there for a moment just feeling it. The weight of it. The implications.

Three surgeries in three years. I could almost hear through the silence the burden falling on his shoulders as he came to the realization that –unless a miracle occurred–our work in Iceland couldn't continue...a work that in many ways had just started.

The phone conversation was difficult and it continued even as I pulled into the driveway and hugged Haley and Darcy with tired, shaky arms.

He wanted to know details.

I couldn't remember details.

My daughters were trying to talk to me at the same time that he was. *Did the doctor open up your tummy and check on the baby? Is she better?*

We talked in short, tight sentences. The lease on the apartment in Iceland was up, so he was packing everything in either storage boxes or suitcases. He would bring his guitar home in case he would need it to pursue positions as a worship leader.

A new job...*it didn't even seem real.*

Even though living in Iceland had been the hardest thing I had ever experienced, it had become home. It was our familiar. It felt like our visa had just come and we had just gotten settled into life there. *Now it seemed like that had all been in vain.*

Colby's voice had a lot of frustration laced through it. I didn't like it, even though I knew I wasn't the source. I went to the back bedroom, behind the door, and gave the tears permission to cascade down the cliffs of my cheeks like waterfalls. Permission for the waterfalls to carve deep.

Permission to feel anything but brave.

11

RIPPLE

---

*"For He regards the prayer of the destitute and does
not despise their prayer."*

Psalm 102:17

May 18th, 2010

I t was my birthday. To celebrate, Colby's Dad drove me
to the DMV to renew my license *even though I had already
tried to do it on the computer.* "I'm just not confident that it
worked..." I kept explaining to him. He graciously drove me
fifty minutes to the closest DMV just so that we could wait in
line for another fifty minutes...*only to find out that I had successfully renewed it online.* "I just didn't trust that it would work..."
I explained to the attendant. Perhaps it was at that moment I
realized I was a *laggard* on the *innovation bell curve.*

Colby's mom and dad left later that day, and as they
pulled out the driveway, I felt more alone than ever. The girls
and I took a quiet walk through the foreign neighborhood,

the whole time my thoughts wandering to what the summer would hold. When we got home, the house felt emptier than ever.

A few short minutes later, our friends Clint and Jennifer knocked on the door. They had gotten me a cell phone to use since all I had was my European Vodafone. I hugged them and thanked them because I hadn't yet thought of that need. They asked about my appointment and we spent the evening together catching up. It felt like my friends were God's literal hands and feet, sent to care for me at the end of a vulnerable day. And I was thankful. Scared, lonely, unsure...but *thankful*.

Blog Post
www.getagarman.blogspot.com
May 21, 2010

Without Daddy

Yesterday morning, I (Annie) went in to Darcy's new bedroom to wake her up (I'm too embarrassed to say what time it was...I guess they we're worn out). She looked so precious, so I just watched her sleep and prayed for her and this whole transition.

*She opened her eyes, stretched out her little arms, found my neck and gave me a classic, tight Darcy hug. After a few moments of cuddling, she asked if she could wake up and sat straight up in bed. Almost immediately, she fell back into a little heap in my arms and started crying...no **wailing,** actually.*

"Darcy...WHAT in the world is wrong, honey?"
She looked up with the most pitiful expression of sor-
row and pain.

"I just can't live without Daddy ANY LONGER."
She collapsed onto my lap again.

"Oh, honey....I know it's hard," I empathized.

"I can't live WITHOUT SILLINESS any lon-
ger," she continued.

"Oh, baby...Well, I can be silly!" I tried to do
a face that only Colby can do. Apparently that only
made matters worse and the cries became louder.
"No!!!....You cannot be silly like Daddy!" I gave up
and just held her instead.

Can everyone please say a quick prayer today that
the volcano will not act up again and that the airport
will be open on the day Colby leaves? We REALLY
need him on this side of the ocean!

✎

The next few weeks passed long. We visited Civil War battlefields quiet and somber, played in the warm and inviting spring rain, explored our temporary home west of Fredericksburg, and welcomed Daddy home from his flight across the ocean.

The Sunday after Colby returned safely to us, our whole family sat together in a back pew at Stafford Baptist Church. People turned and waved during the opening song. We had returned. Back to the church where it had all started. Haley and Darcy looked around with wide eyes, remembering the church they were raised in. I put my arms around their little bodies and held them close, thankful they were handling the transitions so well.

At the end of the service as bulletins rustled and Bibles were being zipped, Pastor Bill asked the congregation to gather around us to pray for our baby. As some stood up to put a hand on our shoulders (and others shifted uncomfortably in their seats), he asked if we had yet picked out a name for our child.

Colby and I looked at each other as we tried to decide with our eyes what to say. The name was supposed to be a secret. *Just like the gender.*

Finally Colby looked forward and announced, "Gracie. **Gracie Garman.**"

I looked down, noticed a crusted drop of yogurt on my black shirt and tried to scratch it off with my fingernail.

It was okay.

Now there was a name to lift with their prayers. Now, a *name* that could ring throughout the throne room of heaven. *It was okay.* She had a name. They could use it.

There was a reverent hush in the silence before the first person prayed and I wondered if God was going to do a miracle that day in my womb. Was it a waste of my time asking and praying for it? *It was as though I'd rather **not even ask** as to **not get my hopes up**. I closed my eyes out of respect, but my thoughts were loud and distracting.*

Did these prayers really matter? What about Summer and Jeremy's baby? Thousands and thousands of people were praying, begging for healing for Tyson. Surely God had heard. But He had answered with a no. Does God just do whatever He wants or wills in the end? Do our prayers really change anything? Do they really ripple throughout eternity?

It turns out I didn't need to decide on my theology at that moment. Many people in the room, wet with tears and humility asked for healing, strength, and peace… and prayed in my place.

$$\mathscr{D}$$

I sat down on the porch swing on the back deck and put my feet on a child-sized plastic chair. It creaked slightly, but that was the only sound that could be heard. I swung back and forth for a little bit as the okra grew in the garden next to me and the blue jays raced through the highways in the sky. It had been awhile since I had blogged and many friends and family had let me know. I had very little desire to write and make public my private wrestlings.

Would God do a miracle and heal Gracie? I thought about it constantly.

Would she –against the odds--be born with a whole heart? *If not, would she survive?* I tried to not think about that. I knew worrying about it wouldn't change anything.

I opened my computer and decided to blog…to turn my attention to giving thanks instead giving complaint. I had heard about this activity. It was said to be helpful…especially in the valleys.

> *www.getagarman.blogspot.com*
> *June 12th, 2010*
>
> *Today I'm counting my blessings…*
> *I'm very grateful that …*

1. *The Icelandic mid-wife noticed something wrong in the ultrasound.*
2. *We all got out of Reykjavik, Iceland before the ash came wild and thick.*
3. *We have a beautiful, FURNISHED house on a lake in the woods to stay in during this rickety time.*
4. *UVA Children's Hospital is just down the curvy road...less than two hours away.*
5. *Some guy named Francis Fontan figured out how to connect the superior and inferior vena cava to the pulmonary artery back in 1968 and therefore has allowed babies to live with a single left ventricle.*
6. *People have donated dimes and quarters over the years to the Ronald McDonald House and we have the option of staying there for the long recovery in NICU.*
7. *Friends who have become family and family who have become friends are everywhere, surrounding us.*
8. *We are still receiving good insurance.*
9. *Doctors are saying things like, "There are a lot of reasons to be positive about this" instead of "I'm sorry...there's nothing we can do."*
10. *Whether it's worst case scenario or best case scenario, **there is hope in Christ.***

12

NOEL DEVIN

*"Hear my prayer, O LORD; give ears to my pleas
for mercy! In your faithfulness answer me, in your
righteousness."*

Psalm 143:1

It was a humid June morning, thick and heavy to breathe
in. We had enjoyed many outdoor days, but this would be
an indoor day. Ninety degrees by 9 am.

My Uncle Jimmy and Aunt Patti had stayed at our place the
previous night; it was a surprise visit as they made their way
home from Connecticut. Haley and Darcy were awake, hair
matted and wild, sitting on bar stools at the kitchen counter.
Uncle Jimmy had been up since the crack of dawn, riding his
bike around the lake that I'm assuming scorched pink with
sunrise. *But, I wouldn't know.*

I was exhausted. The midsummer heat was beginning to
swell my ankles and my body was getting heavier each day.
Anytime guests stayed in our home, the kids woke up earlier

than usual but were somehow also able to triple their energy level. It was understandable. It was fun to see my aunt and uncle after almost four years.

Colby was making coffee, filling our kitchen with the smell of morning and I felt slightly jealous. Caffeine was never a solution for my tiredness. It only made me nervous, anxious, and nauseous followed by grumpy and groggy.

Uncle Jimmy stood drinking water from his Nalgene bottle, giving me the latest news on Grandma and Grandpa Haley. He had just been with them in Connecticut and was sharing the status of their orchard, their health, their lives.

Haley Jane was listening, asking questions about the peach trees and the jellies and the side of the family from which she was named.

I opened up my computer to look something up while Jimmy was talking. Sunshine was climbing now, giving us the only rays that peeked through the windows all day. Gingham shadows flashed across the cabinets.

Our conversation turned to Grandma Haley's homemade bread and how we would make it with the children that day. After all, we would surely have cabin fever. My motivation was low, but Uncle Jimmy's was high and that was all that was needed.

I glanced down at the computer while Uncle Jimmy talked through each step of the bread baking process. A new message. I clicked on it.

It was a long message, so I skimmed it, making sure to look over at Jimmy occasionally as he talked. We would need to be careful when we put the yeast in with the temperature of the water and I nodded as he talked *but I was no longer listening.*

The message. *It was so strange.*

Colby made his way to my end of the room and I grabbed his arm. Subtly, I pointed at the computer screen. He leaned in to the screen and started reading with his coffee cup in one hand. Uncle Jimmy kept talking.

My body turned to clean up cereal bowls and wash hands and look for yeast in the cabinets, but my mind was still staring at the screen. Trying to make sense of it all.

Jimmy asked where the closest store was. I said I didn't know. He asked me which store I shopped at and I quickly answered, trying to come back to reality. *Yes, there was a store. It was only two miles away. Yes, surely they would have yeast. Yes, we could go. Yes, I just needed to finish my breakfast and get showered and clean things up and get the kids ready and hopefully that wouldn't take too long.* My mind reeled.

Was it a joke?

This couldn't happen. This kind of stuff *didn't* happen.

I tried to protect my heart by not believing it.

It was too much to wrap my head around anyway.

Haley and Darcy were running circles through the small kitchen now, excited by the thought of kneading dough and watching it rise. Noise mixed with excitement, mixed with shock, sprinkled with confusion. It was a recipe I wasn't quite sure would turn out.

I turned to Colby and watched as he finished reading the message. His eyes were squinting, trying to understand what he was reading.

He finished and turned his head to me and shrugged as if to say, "I have no idea either..."

After an exciting morning of watching bread rise and bake, we said good-bye to Jimmy and Patti from our front steps. Haley and Darcy settled down for naptime, and the house became quiet again.

I sat down across from Colby at our desk and opened up the email message we had received that morning. If it really was true, it was unbelievable. *Who would do something like this?* I read the message again, slowly, afraid to believe it.

Annie (and all the Garmans),

My name is Noel Devin. I live in College Station, Texas, and you don't know me from Adam!

I've been harassing a dear friend about starting a blog for months and sending her examples of blogs that praise God by showing how He works every day. She has these beautiful twin boys that I'm so grateful I can call my nephews. In this whole thing I've bounced all over the world reading and rejoicing in how God's working everywhere all the time.

Last week, on Wednesday, I landed on your blog. I'm not sure how I even landed there! I feel like a bit of a voyuer, peering into your lives. At the same time, though, I feel genuinely blessed to have encountered you.

Your family (especially the tiny Garman) has been on my heart. I've been praying about this need to help your family financially.

What I believe God had in mind was more than I could manage on my own and I couldn't see a way.

On October 13, 2009, my grandmother was called Home. She was consumed, her whole life, by an insatiable thirst for the Lord. Then last night, after a week of praying for a way to follow through on what God had laid on my heart about your family, I got a phone call from my mom letting me know that Mammy's estate had been settled.

God's given me the means. Will you allow me the opportunity?

I understand that this is out of the blue and may seem a little bit odd. I'd encourage you to pray about it and to discuss it. It is my fervent hope that you'll feel comfortable with this.

In any event, thank you so much for sharing your story. My family is praying for yours and will continue to do so.

Noel Devin

I looked up at Colby who was already looking at me. "I think God is preparing us for something," I said.

13

GREEN

*"Every word of God is pure: He is a shield to those
that put their trust in him."*

Proverbs 30:5

J uly scorched.

Crisp, brown grass covered the earth as we drove past
farms and vineyards on Route 20. Cows hid in their
barns almost as if to protest.

We were driving back home from UVA hospital in
Charlottesville. I felt a kick...a painful yet beautiful reminder
that life was still there. I pressed her foot--a way to talk back
and say I was still there too--and dislodged it from my rib cage.

She was coming. And coming soon.

It had been a long day at another pediatric cardiology appointment. But, how could I complain? University of Virginia's
Children Hospital had been so kind. They were preparing
us as best as they knew how, bending way beyond what was

expected of them. I was humbled by the genuine concern of Dr. Dan Schneider, Carol Tatum, and the rest of the staff.

But now what?

Gracie was to arrive in the next month, and we lived almost an hour and a half away from the hospital. My other two babies had proved to be impatient, not waiting until their due date. Darcy had come ten whole days early. What if Gracie came early too?

Not only that, but with both my pregnancies I had awoken in the middle of the night with contractions four minutes apart. Both times it was a dramatic race to the hospital, complete with speeding and screaming at my husband. What if it went even faster this time? I couldn't have this baby on the side of the road. Not only that, but I would most likely vomit the entire curvy ride to the hospital if we drove when I was in labor.

We passed Keswick Vineyards as Colby and I discussed all the questions that were unanswered. ...the questions that were hanging in the air.

> *When would we go to Charlottesville to await Gracie's birth?*
> *Where would we stay as we waited for her to come?*
> *Where would we stay during the (likely) surgery?*
> *Where would we stay during Gracie's recovery time?*
> *What if the Ronald McDonald House was full?*
> *Would we really be able to afford living in a hotel indefinitely?*
> *How could we make sure our other two daughters would be with us as much as possible?*

How could we know? What was the best decision?

Colby didn't even pretend to have any answers to the questions I was throwing at him and he voiced a prayer to God asking for help in our situation. I wondered why we hadn't done that sooner.

We got home and unloaded from the car, whiny and tired and thirsty every last one of us.

We all parted ways, the kids to their toys, me to start dinner, Colby to his computer. I stood at the door of the fridge and stared inside. *How was all of this going to work out?*

I tapped my foot on the floor, impatient with myself as I tried to decide what to cook. Spaghetti for dinner. Easy enough. The ground beef was frozen and I started peeling off the icy plastic wrap, wishing I had put more forethought into planning meals.

Having been recently warned of the dangers of gamma rays and microwaves, I tugged at the plastic wrap and hoped that somehow my efforts were being used to decrease the risk of cancer in our family.

While I peeled, I daydreamed. Hadn't God known since the foundations of the earth that our baby would have an imperfect heart and that we would have to move immediately from Iceland to the U.S.? Hadn't He known–planned, even– that we would have an American summer in this lake house as we waited?

Didn't God always take care of us when we needed it? *But…maybe wanting to go to Charlottesville before I went into labor was more of a **want** than a need…I mean, yes, I would throw up on the side of the road, but we would eventually make it there.* I freed the ground beef from the last pieces of plastic, only to realize that the process would have been much simpler if I had thawed it under warm water. *I always seemed to make life harder than it needed to be.*

A laugh came from the other room, not far away. "Oh, wow...Annie, you've got to hear this!"

Colby was in the kitchen now, laptop in hand, starting to read me an email he just received.

> *Colby,*
> *This is Deb from Crozet Baptist Church. It would be a pleasure for you to stay in our mission house as you await the birth of your daughter and her surgeries...*

My jaw dropped.

I leaned over and read the email myself. A church west of Charlottesville had a mission house that we could stay in for as long as we needed. It was only fifteen minutes from the hospital, at the base of the Blue Ridge Mountains. We could go there the last week of July and live there indefinitely as we waited for Gracie to arrive and life to become clear. This solved all of our immediate problems...every single last one of them.

"I had emailed them a few weeks ago, but hadn't heard back from them..." Colby's worry lines were being replaced by trust lines of joy all over his face.

God had seen. God had heard. God had provided. This felt like such a complex problem in a complex situation, but God had taken care of it all in one simple email. God's church was being used as His hands, catching us in our freefall of uncertainty.

I felt for a moment like we were inside the verse Jeremiah 17:7. "Blessed is the man who trusts in the Lord, whose trust IS the Lord. He is like a tree...that does not fear when heat comes, **for its leaves remain green,** and is not anxious in the year of drought, for it does not cease to bear fruit..."

It was as though the leaves of our life were miraculously staying green, even though everywhere around us the grass was crisp and scorched. Colby and I read the email over and over again, smiling and laughing...and as the drought ravaged around us, we tasted the sweet fruit of trust. *Even if it was just a sliver.*

Noel,

Wow, we don't know what to say; we are very excited to hear from you. We're glad our blog has encouraged you...that's an answer to prayer! We would be interested in hearing what you have in mind and what God has laid on your heart in regards to our family... all the while helping you better understand our situation. We would also want to be sure that nothing we've communicated on the blog has created any misunderstandings about what our situation is.

{Jesus, Thank you for the internet and how it can connect total strangers! Thank you for Noel and her desire to minister to your people. Please bless her and her family as she has blessed us with her prayers. Amen}

Hope to hear from you soon,
Annie

Annie,

Thanks so much for responding! I have to confess that this is way out of character for me. I'm typically cautious to a fault. I'm the girl who researched the safety standards of dog crates for my schnauzer. And, frankly, I'm still a little bewildered by the fact that I'm following through on this.

I don't have any notion of the specifics of your situation, financial or otherwise, and don't want to make assumptions. I also don't want, in any way, to imply anything in this. Your business is your business and I'm confident that God's going to continue to give me courage and confidence in this. I don't recall any mention, ever, in your blog about financial burdens or anything of the sort. To the contrary, I'd say the opposite is true: confidence that the Lord provides in His perfect time and manner, which is a belief I cling to every day.

I abhor talking about money, no matter which side of the conversation I find myself on. In any event, I'm prepared, once y'all have had a chance to pray about it, to commit to contributing $10,000 over the next year to help ease any financial needs your family has: medical, housing, travel, mental health days for you, real toothpaste for Haley, whatever.

There are no strings attached, no expectations, and no need for justification. I say over the next year because the settlement will divest quarterly beginning in

July. I'll leave it to y'all to sort out the details regarding delivery if you're led to afford me the opportunity to share.

.

Noel

14

GREAT AWAKENING

"And this is the confidence that we have toward him, that if we ask anything according to his will He hears us."

I John 5:14

July 29th was the hottest day of the entire summer. It was also the day that we moved into the mission house; but first we had another appointment at UVA. After a fairly uneventful ultrasound with Dr. Dan, Colby went to get the car and told me to meet him outside the door. The minute I walked out of the cool hospital, I was slapped in the face with a wave of humidity. I had walked out the wrong door, but unfortunately didn't realize it until I was already half way down the blistering sidewalk. I only had one hundred meters to walk until I got to the spot where Colby and I would meet, but every step was heavy and slow. I felt obese.

Colby finally pulled up and I collapsed into the car. "That was the hottest moment of my entire life." He made a sound that was somewhere between sympathy and *"you're being overly dramatic."*

We had four suitcases in the trunk and drove a few miles west to a small town called Crozet. As soon as we pulled up to the mission house, I smiled. I had always dreamed of having a front porch, and it looked like for the next few months I'd have one. There was a playground in the backyard, a tree house, and even a screened-in back porch.

A car drove down the street and the driver waved. I waved back.

I knew I was going to like Crozet.

The neighbors across the street were especially hospitable, taking an interest in our situation. One warm evening, we sat on their front porch sipping orange juice and talked as our children caught lightening bugs and screamed in delight. The mother of six, who spoke with a beautiful British accent, listened with engagement while we talked. As we got up to leave, she grabbed my arm gently and asked if she could come over later that night and pray with me. She wanted to pray and ask God to heal Gracie.

I said sure, but after we had safely crossed the street, I looked over at Colby and mumbled something to the effect of, "I'm not sure how this is going to go."

There were numerous reasons that I started to feel uncomfortable as we made our way to our front door. Since finding out about Gracie's condition, a few people had assured me that if *I prayed and believed that she would be healed,* God would do it.

This was confusing and therefore unhelpful. Was it that simple? Was there really a formula that went something like "ask + believe = receive." If so, how much belief was enough?

It put a lot of pressure on me to conjure up a belief that God was going to do something that I wasn't convinced *He wanted to do.*

I was remembering when we had invited twenty people to our tiny apartment in Reykjavik before we departed the country and asked everyone to pray for God to heal Gracie's heart. The fetal echo at UVA a few weeks later had revealed His answer was a no.

Undeterred, we had asked many people at our church to pray that God would do a miracle and correct the situation. When our church plant, Pillar Church, asked me if I wanted a baby shower, I declined and asked for a prayer meeting instead. And we did. One Sunday morning everyone had gathered, laid hands on me, and *in lieu of playing "taste the baby food,"* prayed for a baby whose heart would function normally.

I had daydreamed often of a miraculous healing. I imagined Gracie, fresh out of the womb, being checked by a confused and stunned pediatric cardiologist as he tried to explain to me how he had been wrong--dead wrong--the entire time.

I had imagined packing our bags and returning to Iceland as a living testimony to the **power** and **might** of a God *who hears and who heals.* Perhaps our friends who were skeptics would become Christians. Maybe their friends would turn to Christ as well and the tiny country would experience a GREAT AWAKENING, only instead of Jonathan Edwards, it would be with people named Ingibjörg and Guðmundur. *Why wouldn't you want to do that, God?* I reasoned with Him.

After awhile, however, I began to be skeptical about my prayers...the sincerity of them, the motives behind them. Did I want God to heal her *so that I would be **spared** the agony of watching my newborn baby girl wheeled away to the ICU moments*

after she entered the world? Did I pray for healing *so that I would be spared the DISCOMFORT and PAIN of enduring her condition?*
Absolutely.

So...what if...what if God *wanted* me to go through the dark valley of her condition and surgeries? What if He had a plan that didn't include us going back to Iceland? Surely no amount of prayer could trump that.

So, I had stopped asking. God had heard our request many times and was obviously free to heal, but I was done begging Him for something I wasn't even sure was **good** for me.

After walking up the steps to our porch, bathing and tucking in the children, we heard a knock at the door and let our new neighbor in. She must have sensed a twinge of discomfort in my mannerisms, because the next thing she asked was, "Is there anything you'd like to talk about before we pray?"

I exhaled loudly, relieved that she was giving me permission to be completely transparent about such a sensitive topic.

"Sure...this is very kind of you....but, we've had a lot of people pray for her to be healed these past few months." I didn't know this neighbor well at all. I didn't want to offend her, but at the same time I didn't think my heart could handle a prayer service that got my hopes up and in the wrong place.

"Please..." I don't know how I desperate I sounded, "Please don't THANK GOD IN ADVANCE that He's going to heal her as if you *know* what God is going to do." I looked over at my husband to elicit support as I went on with my soliloquy. "We don't know WHAT God is going to choose to do, and it's just hard when people *act like they know.*"

She was quiet and just listened. "Please don't pray that I'll have enough faith to BELIEVE that God will do this miracle... like it all depends on *ME* and how much faith I can conjure up in my heart...That gets so confusing. The Bible teaches we're to ultimately have *faith* in the **character** of God, not faith that he'll do what we want."

She leaned over, gave my leg a compassionate and understanding pat, and quietly said, "Absolutely..."

My husband looked up from his gaze at his feet, relieved that his wife hadn't just offended this neighbor who he would have to live next to for another month. He sighed rather loudly himself.

We had heard many people using the verse Mark 11:24, "Whatever you ask in prayer, believe that you have received it, and it will be yours" out of context.

Yes, we were invited to ask, we were even *told* to ask, *but in no way were we entitled to God answering us the way we thought He should.*

After talking through many issues with this neighbor who was becoming a friend, we prayed until the wee-wee hours of the morning.

After we were done, I wasn't sure if God--who had already made a decision-- had changed his mind, if He was still making His decision, or if the decision had been made since the foundations of the world.

15

BIRTHDAY BOY

"Lord, you have been our dwelling place in all gen-
erations. Before the mountains were brought forth,
or ever you had formed the earth and the world,
from everlasting to everlasting you are God."

Psalms 90:1,2

The weeks were starting to drag on, painfully slow, as I wobbled everywhere in the deep Virginia heat. The gravity of what was about to happen was crouching nearer and nearer.

It was another week and another pediatric cardiology appointment. On this particular day, I had grabbed a big jar of applesauce from the fridge on my way out the door. I knew I would be hungry in less than 90 minutes, and that was the only snack I could find in our house.

At UVA, we sat in the same room where I had my original ultrasound. I listened to the doctors and Colby discuss important things while I ate bites of applesauce right out of the jar. The pediatric cardiology team was explaining what would happen when Gracie came out. She would immediately be put on a medicine called prostaglandin that would sustain her life. By the end of the appointment, the applesauce was almost gone and Dr. Dan asked if we had any questions.

I did have a question, but I wasn't sure how to phrase it.

"I actually do have a question," I said, wiping applesauce off of my knuckles.

"Sure," Dr. Dan responded. "There's no such thing as a stupid question."

I turned my head quickly to see how Colby would respond to that statement. Just a few days previous, we had a "discussion" in which Colby was trying to convince me that there actually **was** such a thing as a stupid question. I gave him an exonerated look and proceeded.

"Okay, well, let's say that God actually does a miracle in my womb and Gracie is born with a whole heart...but you don't know that, so you put her on prostaglandin to sustain her life..."

Everyone is watching me as I dramatically explain this whole hypothetical scenario.

"So...would she still be okay?"

Colby shook his head at my over-analysis.

"Yes, she would still be okay. The prostaglandin wouldn't hurt her," Dr. Dan replied with a smile. "In all my years doing this, no one has ever asked me that question..."

Noel,
This is Annie's husband, Colby. Over the past two
weeks Annie and I have talked, prayed, and sought

some counsel from a friend or two so as to not rush to judgment in the matter that you e-mailed about. We have decided that if you are still interested in going through with this, we would like to accept your offer.

I have always been convinced that God would take care of our needs as we labor to serve Him and He has always done so. I do not know what the needs of the future are going to look like as we approach the August birth, but I trust that this a part of what God is doing to strengthen our faith during this time.

We are very grateful that you would desire to do this and are thankful to God for it. We are also amazed how God continues to use our blog to connect us with people, allow us to minister to others, and be ministered to.

We look forward to hearing from you again soon.
Thanks, Colby, Annie, and the girls

August 9ᵗʰ, 2010

I woke up startled, sat up straight in bed, caught a glimpse of myself in the mirror and immediately fell back on to my pillow in disgust.

"*DARN IT!* I made it through another night without having the baby."

It had been a long week that was getting more and more afflictive by the hour. My mom, the one and only Helen Haley, had flown in from Wisconsin and was there to help whenever the big moment came. We were enjoying the last few days of all being able to fit in one car, being able to all go swimming together and, of course, indulging in Crozet Pizza. I had very little to do and very little to complain about. Except, of course, *that the baby had not yet come and every minute it was getting more and more uncomfortable.*

After going to the bathroom, I grabbed "The Hiding Place," an autobiography of a Holocaust survivor named Corrie Ten Boom and skimmed it in an effort to get my mind off myself and my discomfort. After awhile, I bounced repeatedly on the edge of the bed, contrasting Nazi Germany with Crozet, Virginia, and trying to remember what day it was.

Oh no...*It was August 9th.*

My husband's 31st birthday.

Colby's love language was food and the very thought of cooking or baking something sounded exhausting. I prayed to Jesus that I would go into labor and therefore be relinquished of all birthday *expectations* and *responsibilities.* I bounced harder for a few minutes and uncomfortable, aching cramps started to set it. *Yuck.* I laid back down in bed, trying to think of Corrie Ten Boom and how I should just be thankful that **I wasn't in a concentration camp**, yet fighting feelings of self pity every other minute.

Suddenly, I felt a contraction.

16

SNOWFLAKES

"Some trust in chariots and some in horses, but we trust in the name of the Lord our God."

Psalm 20:7

August 9ᵗʰ, 2010
Approximate time line as recorded in my journal:
6:30 AM: First contraction
7:00 AM: *I go to Colby's bed and wake him by whispering in his ear, "Happy Birthday! I think I'm in labor."*
7:15 AM: *Wake up my mom and grumpily boss her around for half an hour while I lay on the couch moaning. Colby gets the idea to wake the kids up so they can see us off to the hospital.*
7:45 AM: *Haley and Darcy come downstairs with excited smiles on their faces like it's the first day of vacation or like they know their lives are about to*

change or something. Minutes later, the contractions completely stop.

7:55 AM: *Everyone is pacing the house, unsure of what to do next. Haley wants to take Daddy to a coffee shop to get him coffee for his birthday, so they leave. I eat some eggs and apologize to my mom.*

8:20 AM: *Colby runs to the store to buy me orange juice for my dry mouth. Contractions are happening inconsistently every 20-30 minutes.*

9:00 AM: *Colby doesn't know what to do with himself, so he goes for an eight mile run that circles the mission house every mile.*

10:20 AM: *I realize that I'm really going to have to WORK for contractions. Colby returns from his run to find me walking laps around the house and rebukes me, telling me what I really need to do is* **RELAX.**

10:23 AM: *I call the nurse. She tells me to walk. Exonerated, I continue walking laps around the house for an hour.*

11:11AM: *Haley and Darcy announce that today is "Kid's Day" and plan an entire schedule for the day (as if there wasn't enough going on).*

11:48AM: *Haley goes ballistic because I ate an entire box of Mac and Cheese that apparently was intended for "Kid's Day" lunch. I lay down and rest.*

11:49 AM: *Colby busts in the bedroom and rebukes me for relaxing, telling me what I really need to do is* **WALK.**

11:50AM: *I get mad at Colby for telling me what to do. ("Do you HAVE ANY CLUE how to treat a* *women who's in LABOR?!?" His response: "Be nice, baby...It's my birthday.")*

12:14 PM: *Colby goes to the store to buy a replacement Mac and Cheese for Haley's "Kid's Day" (who **plans** these things?) in an effort to get her to stop crying.*

12:28 PM: *After a kind invitation, I attend "Kid Club" (one of the many festivities of "Kid's Day") in the upstairs bedroom with nineteen stuffed animals and dolls. Contractions are still irregular.*

1:30 PM: *I walk around the house and the contractions start to pick up to being seven minutes apart. We're making progress...*

2:10 PM: *Contractions are getting more intense (I'm getting more dramatic) and the kids are watching it all with wide eyes.*

2:30 PM: *The time has come. We hug the kids, and wave as we leave for the hospital. I don't have a single contraction on the car ride.*

2:50 PM: *Arrive at triage. I'm only 4 cm dilated. They won't admit me, but give me a room to wait in while I progress. The nurse says that she'll be back in 30 minutes.*

4:03 PM: *We listen to my "labor play list" on the IPOD as I labor consistently and painfully. Colby prays for me and reads me Scripture as I writhe in pain. The nurse has not come back.*

4:38 PM: *Contractions are INTENSE and very close together. Colby has marks from where I'm squeezing his hand every time a contraction hits. He deserves an award for his patience as he endures my moans and screams.*

4:50 PM: I'm crying--no, weeping--between contractions as I realize how close we are to the unknown.

6:03 PM: I've had enough. Colby tries to talk me out of it, but I open up the door to my room and **FLING** myself into the hallway...where I loudly and unashamedly have a contraction for an office full of nurses and doctors.

The office seems to stop and multiple heads turn in my direction. In a desperate attempt for assistance I yell, "DIDN'T **ANYONE** READ MY BIRTH PLAN? I asked for a BOUNCING BALL and an EPIDURAL! Would someone **PLEASE help** me?"

6:03 PM: A nurse comes over and lets me lean on her chest while I endure another uncensored contraction. She apologizes for the delay (I hope I apologized too), then moves us into a delivery room.

7:00 PM: Epidural. Peace and tranquility...

7:30 PM: I take a nap and watch the screen as the contractions slow down. "God, it's been a rough birthday so far for Colby. Please let the baby come before midnight."

10:50 PM: Staff from the Intensive Care Unit begin to fill the room. Everyone is quiet and can hear the worship music that we're playing in the background. It's about to happen. She's about to come.

10:55 PM: One of the doctors is being jovial, pressuring me to push her out in exactly five minutes so that her birth numbers can be 8/9/10 born at 11:00. I'm making jokes partly because I'm drugged up and partly because **approximately sixteen different people are about to watch me give birth.**

11: 04 PM: I start to push. I feel nothing. Everyone is cheering me on with such excitement it feels like I'm about to win a race.

11:07 PM: Now the conversation turns to trying to push her out at 11:11 PM, so that her birth numbers are even more impressive. One nurse objects by saying that 11:12 would be even better.

11:12 PM: She's out and I hear her soft cry. I sit patiently as they clean her up and check her oxygen levels, listening to the other nurses discuss which clock to use for the official birth time (there are three different clocks in the room). I hold her for almost a full minute before she is whisked away to the Neo-natal Intensive Care Unit.

11:12 PM: I watch Colby break down and sob for the next fifteen minutes...I think it's the first time he's cried about this. I can't cry; there are no tears left. I close my eyes and try to breathe, dreaming about the sixty seconds I saw her face.

2:00 AM

I was having a psychedelic dream that made absolutely no sense at all when Colby touched my arm. "It's time to go."

I tried to sit up in bed and move towards the edge, but my body was still in such atrophy that Colby had to help. He helped heave me into the wheelchair by my bed and pushed me down the hallway into the elevator.

"What do you think is going to happen?" he asked.

The dream was still spinning in my mind and my head was hanging down, unable to compete with the heaviness. Not only was I utterly exhausted from laboring for seventeen hours, but the epidural hadn't worn off yet and my mind was still groggy from all the pain killers. I mumbled something from my stupor as the elevator descended...just enough motion to make me feel like I was on a rollercoaster.

The time had come to find out the status of Gracie's heart. She had been whisked to the NICU minutes after she was born where the doctors put her on a special medicine, prostaglandin, which would keep her heart beating. They had just finished the echocardiogram of her heart and were ready to discuss the results with us.

The results that would determine our future.

The elevator opened and we entered the NICU. I didn't look at my surroundings; I just rested my head on the back of the wheelchair unable to fully engage with my emotions. Colby wheeled me right beside Gracie who was attached to hundreds of wires and cords, but appeared to be breathing normally. It was hard to believe she was mine, even though she had just come out of my body three hours earlier. I didn't really know her, so it was hard to feel anything. I went in close to her face and said *hello*. Her eyebrows furrowed.

The pediatric cardiologist started talking and I fought to keep my eyes open as another dream, uninvited, started taking over my weary mind. Here was the moment we all had been waiting for...*what had God decided to do?* I propped my chin on my hand to keep my head from nodding and watched my husband's face as he took in the news. A strained face. A slight nod confirming that he understood.

I could hear a drum roll in my head as I waited for the punch line. Had the diagnosis all been a mistake? Was she a modern miracle? Was her condition treatable with an out-patient procedure? Was it better? Worse?

I glanced over at Gracie, sleeping soundly in her cradle, bundled with cords. The drama of the moment was complete-ly canceled out by my exhaustion. It was hard to care about anything.

After he finished talking, we stood in silence all looking down at the new bundle. Not sure exactly what this doctor had just said, I cleared my throat and asked the big, clarifying question, "So, does she need three open-heart surgeries?" His words were loud enough to be heard over the dream that was taking me away again, "Yes, absolutely."

Colby and I exchanged looks, and I clarified it just so it could be clear. "I guess we're not going back to Iceland." He looked past my shoulder, his eyes very far away. I didn't feel very surprised. Instead, I felt nauseous. Heavy with an anxi-ety that I could feel collecting like snowflakes over every mus-cle and sinew of my body. And, in some strange way...I felt relieved. *Relieved that there was something to know.*

17

SEVENTH FLOOR

"But we have this treasure in jars of clay, to show that the surpassing power belongs to God and not to us."

2 Corinthians 4:7

I woke up the next morning after a sleep laced with some heavy pain medication called Vicodin. The sleep was, of course, what I like to call "hospital sleep," the kind that is interrupted every few hours by someone needing vital signs or something else checked off their list.

I felt light-headed as I tried to sit up in bed.

I looked around the room. My mom was bringing Haley and Darcy to meet their sister and I wanted to get the room looking decent before they came in. The small act of tidying our toiletries made me want to take a nap.

Colby was engrossed at his computer, typing rapidly as though he was a college kid trying to finish his final paper that was due in the next hour. I looked over his shoulder and saw that he was updating our blog for all our friends and family to read:

www.getagarman.blogpost.com
August 10th

So, what's next?

Immediately after Gracie was born, the pediatric cardiologist did an echocardiogram to get a better look at Gracie's heart. The heart echo confirmed the diagnosis that was given for Gracie while she was in utero. Her pulmonary valve is blocked and the right side of her heart is very small and under-developed.

She will likely have a series of procedures called a "Fontan" beginning with a procedure to make sure her ductus arteriosus remains patent (open). The first procedure will probably be done in a couple of days. It is a temporary procedure that will allow her to grow for a few months before another procedure can be done.

Shorthand: Gracie is healthy right now, but her heart will have to be re-arranged a bit to help her remain healthy. The re-arrangement will probably take three steps in the first couple years of her life.

While we wait for the rest of the plan to come together, we are enjoying our new little bundle and getting ready to introduce her to her very excited sisters.

The next couple hours I focused my thoughts on something other than my feelings and enjoyed taking the kids to the Neo-Natal Intensive Care Unit (NICU) to meet their baby sister. Haley and Darcy looked so grown-up and proud as they signed their names in the guest check-in book, sanitized their hands, and walked over to Gracie.

They smiled wide, and stood on a stool to see their new baby doll sleeping with a furrowed brow in her little plastic box. It was all so soft and beautiful, like a blanket that covered a twinge of sadness...*sadness that they had to meet her like this.* I had to make a conscious decision not to lift up the blanket and peek underneath.

Colby's parents arrived later the next day, as did my Dad who flew in from Wisconsin. Gracie was transferred to the Pediatric Intensive Care Unit (PICU) and we were able to have a "room" of our own, shared with two other patients, but separated by a curtain. Because it was in a corner, we weren't allowed to stay overnight with her in the room. We were all the more thankful for the mission house in Crozet big enough to fit both our families.

Before I knew it, it was time for me to be released from the hospital. I hadn't for one moment thought about what this would feel like.

Annie's Journal
August 11th, 2010

Today I get discharged from the hospital. I'm sitting by my window in a quiet room waiting for the nurse, who is scribbling through a stack of papers. Outside there is a thunderstorm performing on a stage of green with a striking backdrop of blue mountains.
It's really a choice.
I feel like I could go inside myself and weep for endless hours because I'm not bringing my baby home from the hospital today. Or I could lift my head out of my feelings and look around at all the babies fighting for their lives in the Neo Natal Intensive Care Unit, and just be thankful that she's doing well.
I have done both.
Almost simultaneously.

My thoughts were interrupted by the nurse who needed my signature on a trove of papers. I tried to focus on each stroke of the characters in my name, anything to distract me from the self-pity that was crouching at the door.

I took a minute to skim what I was signing. Release papers. They instructed me to not lift heavy objects for the next week, stay hydrated and take it easy. As I carried my three bags down the hallway to the elevator, I rolled my eyes in annoyance that I had to lift things I had just pledged not to. For a moment, I gave in to self-pity. Colby was with his parents and our older daughters, and we would all be together soon, but for the next few minutes, I was alone in the hospital.

It felt so unnatural. My baby was out of my body, but not in my arms. To leave the hospital without her felt like I had lost her, even though she was in stable condition on the seventh floor. I tried to stop the tears by reminding myself she was still alive, but slid almost immediately into the mire of disappointment.

It made me motion sick to ride the emotional teeter-totter, up and down…striving to look up and be thankful, but the gravity of the trial tugging at my eyelids, making it hard to keep perspective. I sat down in the hallway of the hospital to fight the dizziness and regain my balance. After all, I had signed the release paper promising to take care of myself.

www.getagarman.blogspot.com
August 12th

Surgery Date

*First Off, I (Colby) have neglected to give all the essentials details that people ask for when a baby is born. So here goes: **Gracie Kane Garman** was born at 11:12PM on August 9th, 2010. She weighed 7lbs. 3 oz (that's 3.25 kg for my Icelandic friends) and was 20 inches long.*

The doctors have scheduled Gracie's first surgery for Tuesday at 12:00PM. She will have a BT

(Blalock-Taussig) Shunt surgically installed between the aorta and the pulmonary artery, as well as a little procedure done on her atrial septum. It is the first surgery in a series of three surgeries called a Fontan procedure. The second surgery will be at the 4-6 month timeframe and the third somewhere around three years.

The surgery will take 2-3 hours and is pretty much a miracle of modern medicine. The doctors will be placing a 3.5mm shunt on ridiculously small arteries and sewing it on with thread that is not visible to the naked eye. Her heart itself is only the size of a plumb. The surgery will be open-heart and she will have to go on a blood bypass, so it is a pretty intense deal.

We are so thankful for the great team of doctors and surgeons here at UVA that have helped us prepare for the upcoming week. We really feel like God has directed us to a great place where we can feel as comfortable as possible with this vulnerable situation. We have certainly sensed God's sustaining grace in the past few days and have really been able to enjoy seeing our little girl without feeling overwhelmed with anxiety and fears.

Thank you to all of you who have prayed for us these past few days and for all of the kind words of encouragement and celebration. Please continue to pray for little Gracie and the rest of the family as we get ready for Tuesday.

I read Colby's blog post as I brushed my teeth back at the mission house. I thought about his words as I turned off my lamp and pulled the covers over my head. God had definitely sustained us and I whispered a thank you to Him for all the little prayers He had answered. She had (just barely) been born on Colby's birthday, her color was good (I had been afraid she would come out blue), and she was in stable condition.

God's peace and presence during the last few days had been almost palpable. Being released from the hospital had been a horrible couple of hours, but for the most part, there was a lot of joy and gratitude in our room on the seventh floor. The fears and anxieties were there, that was true. But, God was there too and I knew He was bigger. Some days I remembered this well. *Other days, I was a little more forgetful...*

18

WHATEVER HAPPENS

"We are afflicted in every way, but not crushed; perplexed but not driven to despair; persecuted, but not forsaken; struck down but not destroyed..."

2 Corinthians 4:8,9

The day before Gracie's surgery, I woke up with a strange feeling of sickness mixed with peace. I'm not sure why, but I began to feel a strong temptation to run away...*away from everyone*. There were so many emotions that I was experiencing and I just wanted to deal with them alone.

I was told to be at the hospital at 2:30 for the pre-operation meeting... at 2:34, I was still trying to find a parking spot. Turns out it didn't matter. It wasn't until 4:15 that our pediatric nurse practitioner came in to our room, apologizing for the delay. We had met her earlier in the week and had clicked immediately with her Mid-West accent, humor and charm.

I affectionately had been referring to her as "Lady Chamberlain" because the name sounded like it could be a character in Mister Roger's Neighborhood. It didn't make sense, but I guess it was my way of coping with stress. Making up nicknames for people, trying to make them laugh, trying to make the atmosphere less heavy and more jovial.

After a few minutes of joking and reminiscing about Wisconsin together, she opened her bag and took out a series of thick charts bound together. I started to squirm as the atmosphere in the room changed along with the expressions on her face.

"Tomorrow's surgery is a pretty serious one, and I have to take you through the risks before you sign the release form." I don't think she got any more sentences in before I stood up, asking to be excused from the party. I hadn't been sure if I could stomach this meeting, and now I was sure.

Absolutely sure.

Colby was already prepared for me to react like this, but Lady Chamberlain looked confused. I gathered my things, explaining that I couldn't handle hearing every single last possible thing that could go wrong during the surgery. I already had enough material to work with for my fears and anxieties and dreams and nightmares. *Could I just come back in twenty minutes to sign my name and my life and my daughter's life away?*

She understood. Perhaps she had encountered other people who responded to stress this way. I walked quickly down the hall of the PICU, as though I was running away from my tears that were following me, chasing me every step of the way. The automatic doors opened and I fled the PICU as though it was on fire.

Waiting at the door of the elevator, there was nothing to do to hide my brittle condition, and a doctor waiting next to me asked if everything was okay. I looked down at her nametag and tried to hide my surprise. This was an *anesthesiologist*, not a licensed counselor, yet here she was, caring and showing genuine concern. The elevator came and went, but she stood listening to me as I talked in a choked up voice.

"Tomorrow they are going to stop my baby's heart so they can open it up..." the words were barely intelligible as I poured my heart out to a complete stranger. "I feel like we are standing at death's door with our daughter in our arms...and there's absolutely nothing we can do. It's just up to God...and I don't know what He's going to do. I'm having trouble trusting that He's going to make a good decision."

She listened intently, nodding her head, waiting until I was done. "Okay, well...first of all, I don't think she's necessarily at death's door." She said it very academically and objectively. I wiped away the tears and mucus with my sleeve. "We stopped seventy hearts at this hospital today. We do it all the time. It sounds scary, but the surgeons really know what they're doing."

She continued to listen as we waded through all of the fears and risks together. Maybe it was her surgical facemask and her scrubs that covered her head all the way down to her toes. Talking to her was like talking to an anonymous online counselor or a priest hidden behind a window. She was real and present, but just *anonymous enough* to be completely vulnerable with. We talked for a while. Eventually she might have even hugged me. It's hard to remember, but eventually she got on the elevator and I thanked her.

I stood still for a while praying for strength, and finally mustered up enough of it to go back to our room. When I saw Colby, his face was a shade of white I had never seen him wear. Eventually, I signed my blurry name.

We called my parents to check in with them as they were taking care of Haley and Darcy for the entire day. The kids were doing fine, but were apparently horrified by the meal that someone had generously dropped off for dinner. *Crab Macaroni and Cheese*. It appeared not even a looming open-heart surgery for their baby sister was enough to distract them from the horrors of fake seafood.

Colby held my hand as we left the PICU to get some dinner, both of us feeling like we had been drained of all the life in us. Deeply absorbed in my own feelings and fears, I selfishly asked Colby if I could skip being at the surgery the next day. I just wanted to run away. *Far, far away.* Deep into the bosoms of the mountains where I could cry loudly and no one would hear me. I had convinced myself that I couldn't handle being at the hospital, but was completely oblivious to my husband's needs and desires.

Colby wasn't even sure if it was a good idea. *What if something went wrong? Wouldn't I want to be there?* Of course, this made matters even worse. *Do you THINK something is going to go wrong? Why are you talking like this?* We sat in the parking lot of Barracks Road Shopping Center for a really long time, both of us so hyper-sensitive that every comment was taken as a personal attack.

It was such a low point, that moment in the hot car with the heat rising in our veins and in our words and in the August sun. I couldn't see straight. I couldn't see or think about anything but my overwhelming feelings. And I especially couldn't see how my desires to *not be at the surgery* were making Colby feel completely alone.

We walked into a crowded Panera and stood next to each other, staring up at the menu. Colby spoke, maybe trying to ease the tension or set his mind straight, but either way, his words hushed me. "Ultimately her days are numbered. God knows how many days she has." It was such a strong statement...I didn't even know what to say.

It made hot tears come to my eyes and yet it comforted me all at the same time.

We sat down, but I couldn't even eat my Creamy Tomato soup, my throat was so tight. Mustering up enough strength to work my jaw and chew the asiago cheese croutons felt overwhelming.

After talking about what to do next, we decided to go back to the hospital. The room was very quiet as we stood over Gracie's bed. My mind was consumed with myself, leaving Colby to bear the weight of the moment alone.

It was as though I was getting ready in my heart to say goodbye to my daughter, trying to prepare myself for the worst. It made the night intensely emotional.

I was about to leave, still unsure of my plan for the next morning, when a nurse came in to our room announcing there were visitors to see us. We looked at each other in confusion. We didn't know of anyone coming into town to see us.

I started to feel a little annoyed. We weren't in the mood to see anyone. More than that, *we weren't sure if anyone could enter into the moment with us.* We walked to the entrance of the PICU, a little battle weary. When the automatic doors opened for us, we both stopped, frozen with shock. Immediately Colby started crying and that rare occurrence made it even harder for me to hold back my tears.

It was Jeremy and Summer.

Jeremy embraced Colby and Summer held me as they both let us cry on their shoulders for a really, really long time.

It had been years since we'd seen them, but standing with them there, it was as if it had only been a few days. They had just heard about our little Gracie through the trickle of social media, and without even stopping to find phone numbers and call us, they hopped in their van and drove to the hospital, confident that it was the right thing to do.

As Summer hugged me tight, no emotions were held back. *I let it all out.* But, it didn't intimidate her; she held tighter as though she were weathering a storm, not letting go of the helm.

Eventually we were interrupted by a chaplain who came up to check on us. *Had something just happened? Did we need him to pray?* We started laughing through our tears and explained that we were all old friends who hadn't seen each other in a really long time.

I was in shock…it was almost as if God had sent them directly to us. I had thought of them numerous times in the past nine months since they had lost Tyson. I knew they were in a unique position to understand.

After gathering some of our composure, they followed us back to our room in the PICU. We all sanitized our hands and softly approached Gracie's bed as she slept. Tears dripped down onto her striped blanket as I stroked her little cheek and Summer rubbed my back to comfort me.

"When we heard that Gracie was having surgery tomorrow, we felt a really strong pull to drop everything that was going on and come to see you guys," Summer whispered, looking down at Gracie and then at us. "We wanted to come here tonight to tell you...**It will be okay.**" Summer said it smoothly, as one who knew.

I furrowed my brows.

I had heard that statement a lot in the last few months, and—though meant to comfort me-- it really just confused me. It felt almost like a worthless statement. *It will ALL be OKAY?* Everyone who said this—were they claiming to be fortune-tellers? Had they been to the future and come back to tell me that things were going to be fine? On what basis did they know the surgery would go perfectly?

"Really?....." I probably sounded critical. "But...*how can you say that?*"

Summer didn't mind my push back. In fact, she spoke with a firmer voice and an even greater confidence. "Because... WHATEVER HAPPENS, *it will be okay.*"

I stopped long enough to look at her in the eyes. This thought was a new one.

Things would be okay...*regardless* of how it all went down? How was *that* possible?

"WHATEVER happens, **it will be okay**...*because God will take care of you.*"

I let her words sink in...trickle down to deep parts of my soul that were dry and crusty. And then I remembered how God had whispered the same thing to me in the days following the ultrasound.

How could I argue with this woman who had been through the valley of the shadow and come back to testify? If anyone could make that statement, she could. If anyone could get me to *stop long enough to consider,* it was her. She had earned the badge, the degree, the license. She spoke from experience. She had passed the test.

She went on to explain how, even as they stared death in the eyes, God had sent a peace that was clearly supernatural. God's presence, not their circumstances, sustained them in the months following the loss of their son.

It would be okay? I hadn't understood, *but now I was beginning to.* I was beginning to see Jesus in the fog of the unknown future. I was starting to get how my theology and what I believed about God could actually shape what I was experiencing.

After all, this Christian faith *that I claimed to believe* taught that believers in Christ had hope. A hope so secure and un-believable that it actually could give joy (Romans 15:13). A hope that our trials weren't in vain and were working to grow us (James 1:2-3). A hope of a life beyond this one (Titus 3:7).

The night was just getting started, even though it was getting close to my bedtime. We listened to our friends well into the night...story after story in which God was the hero, sweeping in to save the day, even in the most desperate of circumstances.

We listened to their tale of Tyson's final morning and how, as his Daddy carried his lifeless body to the hearse, snow be-gan to lightly fall out of the bright, white sky almost as though heaven and earth collided for a brief, other-worldly moment. They told of the joys along the painful journey, and how God showered so much love, the cup that was given them became palatable. We sat, humbled.

As the night stretched on I began to feel fear losing its grip on me. It was as though God had sent two witnesses who had stared down death to speak truth to me. The truth was that *in Christ we had hope.* Hope that He would bring us through whatever He decided to take us through, and a greater hope that someday all wrongs would be made right.

The next day loomed ahead of us, like a giant wall that kept growing, but now it didn't seem impossible to climb. I looked down and saw harnesses, ropes, carabiners, climbing shoes and helmets that God had seemed to drop off while I wasn't looking. Funny how He does that.

Almost like He's real and involved...*or something crazy like that...*

19

CROWD SURFING

"For this slight, momentary affliction is preparing for us an eternal weight of glory beyond all comparison."

2 Corinthians 4:17

August 18th, 2010
Charlottesville, VA

I arrived at the hospital around nine in the morning. When I arrived, Jeremy was in the waiting room with Colby, acting as a surrogate helpmeet, which I both felt ashamed and thankful for.

Colby had slept over at the hospital in the cot room the night before so that he could be there to hand her over to the surgeons at 8:00 AM (an activity we decided best that I *didn't* participate in). As the three of us talked, another couple walked in to the small room and sat down.

After awhile we started talking and discovered they had just had a baby a few days after Gracie was born. Darryl, their baby boy, had the same heart defect as our Gracie. The nurses had been referring to them as twins since they were going to be having surgery on the same day.

There was an instant connection between our families. We shared our stories and our unique experiences that were so similar. The twenty-week ultrasound. A tumultuous third trimester. Delivery day. We conversed all day long and I think it helped both of us knowing that we weren't alone. When the moments lulled, they focused their spare attention on a 5,000 piece puzzle that was strewn across a table like a map of uncharted territory.

Throughout the morning I escaped periodically to lay down in the cot room, write, pray, and breathe slowly. There was so much adrenaline rushing through my post-childbirth body, I felt moments from vomiting all day. I hated that I wasn't in control. At the same time, it was kind of nice to not be in control. As my best friend Melissa had put it, "At least YOU don't have to be there in the operating room, performing the surgery."

Mid-morning, I excused myself so I could write a blog post for friends and family who were following our situation from afar.

www.getagarman.blogspot.com
August 18th, 2010

The Day

Right now Gracie is in open-heart surgery. Anticipating this moment was worse than the actual moment. Last night we met with the doctors and had a Pre-Operation meeting where they go over everything *that could possibly go wrong. It was so brutal that I (Annie) had to leave **before it even started**. When Colby walked out of the meeting, he had lost most of the color in his face and lips.*

So, today I decided to write a book. Someone told me recently that they were very disappointed how little I've written about this experience. It has been almost too emotional and personal to share via the blog, but I realize now that some people could benefit from my words. I'm feeling like the ONLY way I know how to deal with this is through writing, so I might as well make it available to others who are going through similar difficulties. More on this topic later...

This morning I woke up at 3:30am and couldn't go back to sleep, so I drove into the mountains on Skyline Drive (ten minutes from the mission house). I watched the stars melt away into colors of early dawn. I didn't put on any music or even pray out loud to Jesus. It was too solemn and sacred of a moment to even speak.

For my ride down the mountain, I listened to a cd of the gospel of Mark. I listened to the life of Jesus, amazed that a man who lived over 2000 years ago could make such an impact on history and on my life today. I don't get it sometimes...all I know is that it's true.

I'm at the hospital now. There is a sign right outside this door in the hallway that says, "UVA MEDICAL CENTER....Good Outcomes Are in Our Hands." I appreciate UVA and all they're doing right now. But, Gracie's life is not ultimately in UVA's hands. It's not in the surgeon's hands. Gracie's life has been and always will be in God's hands.

Thank you Jesus that we can rest in you...the author of life.

Throughout the morning, more and more visitors accumulated in the waiting room. Soon the waiting room was packed with friends and family, almost like a bad, nervous party that no one wanted to be at, but that everyone felt obligated to attend.

Hundreds of people were praying for us, for Gracie, *for grace*, which was a good thing since my prayers were usually an average of three words before they got jumbled and distracted and weary. I could feel the prayers of God's people almost physically during this time. "It feels kind of like *crowd-surfing*," I kept saying to describe what I was feeling. We were going through the trial, but not like I had imagined....it was as though *everyone's prayers had turned into arms and we were being carried along by them.* There was really no other explanation for how we were functioning.

There were so many messages to read through, and they were a good diversion for the soul. My personal favorites were prayers that people would write out and send as a message. I could hear their prayers for us and participate in them without having to conjure up the words myself.

The surgery was long and longer and longest. But, there were many people to talk to and listening to them pulled me up out of myself just far enough to reach oxygen level.

The worst parts were when the surgeon would call Colby's cell phone, and I would have to watch every flinch of my husband's forehead and eyebrows as he listened to the report, but not knowing what they meant. I would try to cram in close to his ear, but never successfully enough to hear for myself.

Finally the moment came. I was talking to my Dad on my phone when I saw our surgeon coming down the hallway, walking slowly towards me. We caught each other's eyes and I couldn't bear the suspense as he finished his walk of thirty yards to me. I quickly flashed him a thumbs-up sign, *as though to ask the gravest of questions in the most elementary of ways.* He graciously popped up his thumb, playing along with my game and I let out a sigh of relief loud enough for my Dad to hear on the phone.

The surgeon strutted up to me, very jovial, and I had to restrain myself from giving him a hug. I think I squeezed his arm, trying to show appreciation and gratitude for his work. We walked in to the waiting room together where I was happy to watch everyone's faces as they got to hear the news of how well the surgery went. Colby looked like he was about to collapse with relief *like a 16th century woman whose corset had just been removed.*

The surgeon proceeded to tell us the next steps which included getting her to breath on her own and removing the chest tube. Colby gathered the whole room together to give a prayer of thanks to God. And then we all walked down the hallway to dinner with such normalcy that it almost felt wrong.

20

STARTING BLOCKS

*"O Lord, you hear the desire of the afflicted; you will
strengthen their heart; you will incline your ear."*

Psalm 10:17

My friend Jennifer walked beside me and asked how I was feeling as we made our way to dinner. "Are you relieved that she made it through the surgery… or are you still nervous about the recovery?"

What came out of my mouth next was a complete shock to me. "She'll be fine," I said so casually and confidently that I wondered why on earth I hadn't believed it earlier.

I continued, sharing something that we hadn't shared with anyone. "When we were in Iceland, we invited all our friends over to pray for Gracie to be healed. While we were praying, my friend Agnes had a vision of Gracie as a fit and healthy teenager in work-out clothes. She described her in starting blocks, getting ready for a race. Agnes wanted to be careful with my heart, so she wasn't claiming to know whether or not this was really a vision from God.

She had experienced many people abusing this kind of thing in the past, saying that God was showing them something He really wasn't showing them…and she just wanted to be so careful. But just last week, Cindy told me that she had a dream about Gracie and it was really similar. I don't know…*I think Gracie's going to do just fine.*"

Jennifer and I both listened to the words coming out of my mouth. Yes, we had invited all of our friends over to pray for Gracie before we left Iceland. Yes, Agnes had looked up at the end of our prayer time and cautiously shared what she had seen while she prayed. Yes, I was cautious to believe her because *who knew if it was just an optimistic daydream or a message from God.*

But here I was, five months later, suddenly and completely confident that God was going to preserve her life for years to come.

Time would tell, but for that moment, I felt like I was given strength to believe that God had spoken through Agnes that day. I had been afraid to believe it, but maybe, just maybe, this vision had been a gift. An unexplainable gift. We walked to Qdoba and I felt spoiled in every way by a Heavenly Father who was proving Himself to be present, personal, and involved.

I went back to the waiting room later that afternoon to look for a book I'd lost. I opened the door as I was finishing a conversation with someone in the hallway, so my loud, exuberant voice carried into the waiting room rather abruptly. Darryl's parents were speaking with the pediatric cardiologist and I clearly had just busted in on a very serious moment.

Everyone looked over at me, and I quickly apologized for the loud interruption. As I was on my hands and knees looking for my book under some chairs, I heard the words, "We'll continue to monitor things, but we have found some severe complications..."

I stayed still as I heard what was unfolding on the other side of the room. The doctor gave a stoic apology and exited. The parents held each other for a few somber minutes, then numbly went back to their puzzle and worked in silence. I swallowed hard, and eventually stood up to face them.

I asked them how Darryl was doing, but it was clear from their expression that it wasn't good and that they weren't ready to talk. My light, sense of relief had collided with their sense of gravity and the two didn't seem to mix well in the same cup. I left the room quickly, embarrassed that I had even been there.

Gracie continued to recover well even though she looked like she had just been in a traumatic car accident. It was incredibly emotional to see her in that brittle condition. I had to just trust the nurses and not my feelings that she was at death's door.

The day after her surgery, my parents flew back to Wisconsin and all our visitors left. Haley and Darcy were picked up by a friend to go to Pennsylvania where Colby's sister, Brooke, was getting married. It felt like the calm after the storm. *We had made it through the hard part,* so we thought. Maybe you've heard it said that *expectations are everything.* Apparently, our expectations for the next few days were a little off...

ॐ

Blog Post
www.getagarman.blogspot.com
August 20th, 2010

The Crash (You Should Know About It)

Annie and I consider ourselves observers.

We observe everything we can...smells, sights, people, accents, our children, personalities, and of course, our favorite...idiosyncrasies (ours and others). We love to find patterns in things and anticipate things, maybe to a disagreeable fault.

Over the past two years, amidst our various crazy times, we have observed a pattern that is now unmistakable. It's called **The Crash.** *Most of you who are more intelligent than us probably already know about "the crash," but I am totally amazed to see how consistent it is. Every high adrenaline/intensely stressful experience seems to be followed by the dearly beloved* **adrenal nosedive.**

Symptoms of the crash include: hyper-sensitivity, temporary irrationality, low-energy, moodiness, magnification, weepiness, and just being ridiculous.

As of Wednesday night we had gotten over the huge surgery day, Annie's parents headed to the airport, Haley and Darcy were on their way to Aunt Brookie's wedding weekend, and it was just Annie and I with Gracie.

Needless to say Thursday morning we woke up to the "The Crash" and stumbled our way through the day, happy to bid it farewell.

So why do I tell you all this personal baloney? It's not because we want to garner your sympathy and concern. Someday, when I look back at the blog I don't want to feel like we ignored the bumps and bruises of the territory. I don't want people who read and follow our journey to see our smiling pictures and think that we haven't had our sketchy moments.

Furthermore, when we write about the joys and celebrations I want you to be able to take them seriously, knowing that we have been honest about the hard parts.

Sitting here today — this side of the crash — we celebrate how gracious God has been to sustain us through the past ten days. We have had more to celebrate than to fear. Gracie is breathing on her own,

without a tube in her nose. She looks peaceful and on
the way to recovery.

I read Colby's blog post and smiled. He had left out the juicy details of our date night that went south...details such as me losing my temper and getting out of our car at a red light *and Colby being found sitting dejected on a street corner by our friends Kyle and Christine.* I sighed. It was probably for the best. He was being as transparent as he knew how to be.

Stress had the potential to strain your marriage...*that was the point.*

21

STAYIN' ALIVE

"As we look NOT to the things that are seen, but to the things that are unseen. For the things that are seen are transient, but the things that are unseen are eternal."

2 Corinthians 4:18

L ife in the PICU ticked along as well as it could. Colby and I recovered from "the crash" and apologized to each other for our various sin issues. Even though Gracie *looked* like she was fighting for her life, the nurses kept convincing me that she was doing well. I was learning how to focus on the facts rather than my feelings.

Colby spent many hours of his day working on his resume and sending it to churches. Occasionally he would ask, "What do you think about Vermont?" or some other random state. I wasn't so sure. I was falling in love with Charlottesville and didn't want to leave. Unfortunately, the only job Colby could find in Charlottesville was a UPS driver, and I wasn't ready to go back to teaching full-time. Besides, the school year was starting that very week.

Haley and Darcy loved life in the PICU. The hospital provided a little class for them to go to in the mornings, so they had someone focusing on them, doing crafts and activities with them while we were with Gracie in the room. It was a lifesaver for us as all our friends and family were gone. The kids were happy as long as we were happy.

On one particular day, my old college roommates, Heather and Tracy, drove to visit us and stayed through lunch. They brought with them a lightweight atmosphere and I enjoyed basking in it. After lunch, we got in the elevator and rode to the seventh floor, laughing about something. When our elevator doors opened, lights were flashing, alerting and alarming us that all was not well. Some kind of emergency was happening and no one was allowed in the PICU.

The entire mood changed as soon as we stepped off the elevator. Heather held my arm and Tracy came in close to me as though she was shielding me from an explosion that was happening in our proximity. I leaned my head on the wall closest to me as I started to feel light-headed.

A nurse came out and whispered to me that it wasn't my baby, so an awful sense of relief mixed with horror washed over me. It wasn't happening to me, but it was still happening to *someone*. I closed my eyes and prayed. No tears emerged, but I cried a shaky, panting cry. The colorful blocks that patterned the floor seemed to spin out of control.

After a few minutes of somber waiting, a young resident pediatric cardiologist shot out of the PICU door, his eyes looking frantic. For one brief moment he paused, our eyes locked, and I saw wet helplessness in them. Neither of us said anything. He ran down the hall.

𝔔

In one of the days following Gracie's surgery, I took a walk down the hall to get a break from the beeping of life-sustaining machines in Gracie's room. Darryl must have been having a procedure done, because his Grandma was in the waiting room.

Our relationship seemed to be established enough, so I felt the permission to walk into the room and give Grandma a hug. I asked if I could pray for her and as I did, tears rolled down her face. She started to get a little hysterical, and I don't remember how or why, but I just suddenly had the confidence to speak firmly and confidently, **"This is not in your hands. This is in God's hands."**

After I said it, her crying quieted a little and I found myself surprised. This idea seemed to calm her down, but the very moment the words left my mouth, I wasn't so sure that it was comforting *to me*. **God would ultimately decide what to do with Gracie's life and Darryl's life and it wasn't up to us...** *Was that thought comforting or maddening?*

We sat there for a few minutes in silence as I wrestled with the idea of God's sovereignty. I asked if I could pray with her, and as I did I felt like a hypocrite. Here, I was trying to minister hope to this woman by pointing her to God, but at my core I was wrestling with whether or not this God was good. I knew He was, but at the exact same time, I didn't know if He was.

In my sheltered life, I had never spent time in a hospital. For the first time, my theology was hitting the pavement of sickness and suffering and it was not exactly a smooth landing.

In the end, I knew there were two choices. I knew the choices were to either *trust Him* or *be angry at Him because I couldn't understand it all.* In this particular moment, I stood suspended between the two, unable to rest securely in either one.

The days started to go by quickly since we had a routine: get kids to UVA children's program, feed Gracie, eat lunch, feed Gracie, rest while Colby scrolled through churchstaffing.com. The day the nurse came in and told us we could take Gracie home, I almost wet my pants. *Bring her home?* It was almost as if I had forgotten that was the end goal.

Hearing how close we were to the finish line made me feel more nervous than I'd been. *Did I really know what to do in every situation? How would I know when to call an ambulance? What if I overreacted and called 911 when I should have just remained calm and called a doctor?* After all, making unnecessary trips to the hospital could be costly.

That day, I sat by Gracie's bedside while she napped. A nurse happened to be in the room and we were chatting about all my questions when it happened. The monitors showed a flat line due to sleep apnea. The machines started beeping like crazy and the nurse leaned in close to Gracie to check her breathing. After a few seconds, the heart rate began to rise and fall like normal, but I burst into adamant tears anyway.

"See?!" I exclaimed *as though to show her that my fears weren't far-fetched and ridiculous.* "What am I supposed to do if that happens at home? I'm NEVER going to be able to sleep! I'm going to be so worried about her!" My sobs were loud and honest.

She got in close to my face *so that I wouldn't forget* and sternly instructed me otherwise. "What just happened is normal. Everyone does this while they sleep. You CAN take care of her...Don't tell yourself that you can't!"

She was like a strict early century schoolmaster and I half expected her to pull out a switch and swat my fingers. It was like she was meeting my intensity with intensity because that was the only way I would hear. This nurse was strong and she knew I needed confidence in my parenting.

Later that day we went to a CPR class where we practiced life-saving procedures on a rubber doll. I tried to make the atmosphere more light by singing "Stayin' Alive" while we did heart palpitations, *but no one seemed very amused.* I didn't blame them. We were learning various scenarios in which to keep our baby alive while we waited for an ambulance to arrive.

Even though I didn't think I was prepared to care for Gracie, the UVA PICU staff seemed to think so. Our pediatric cardiologist, Dr. Dan, was so calm and relaxed. I had hundreds of questions, but he answered most of them with the same six words: *Treat her like a normal baby.*

Meanwhile, baby Darryl was still fighting for his life. He had made some progress at first, but then took a turn later in the week. On our last day in the hospital, we went in his room to see him. His chest was open and you could see his heart pulsating through the clear tape. It was unreal. I watched for a long time as the tape rose and fell and contemplated how

God uses such a small organ to sustain life. *Life is unfathomable when you really take the time to think about it.*

www.getagarman.blogspot.com
August 25th, 2010

Stepping Out...

...of the hospital that is. Tonight is a daddy-daughter sleepover at the hospital. In order to be released, we had to be responsible for Gracie with all of her little details for an entire day. So I (Colby) am staying the night here with Gracie and getting us ready for the big release day tomorrow.

In preparation for her release we had to be trained on giving her meds, using the pulse oxymeter (which we will be taking home with us), and our new baby scale. We took a CPR course and covered all the what-to-do-when possibilities that one could possibly handle in a short period of time. She is a little bit less than her birth weight, but is eating two ounces every three hours.

The bottom line is Gracie will be leaving the hospital tomorrow only 9 days after major open-heart surgery and 17 days after she was born. We are so grateful. She has really recovered at best-case scenario speed.
-Colby

22

DINNER PARTY

"How precious is your steadfast love, O God! The children of mankind take refuge in the shadow of your wings."

Psalm 36:7

August 26th, 2010
Charlottesville, VA

"I think someone's ready to go home," a sweet nurse with a charming southern accent looked over at me as she took Gracie's vital signs. I was smiling so big my cheeks started to hurt. The nurse removed the final cord that had bound Gracie to her bed and handed her to me. *For the first time, I held a wireless baby Gracie.*

Darcy snuggled in close, giving her new sister her first Eskimo kiss. Haley's eyes were bright and full, as if they were smiling themselves. Everyone's faces were fresh and colorful, painted with new joy. It was almost like we were all meeting her for the first time...seventeen days after her birth. Colby came in, slightly sweaty after making multiple trips to the car with all our stuff. He smiled at the reunion unfolding before his eyes.

I packed all six pounds of her tiny body tightly and securely into her carrier and we carried her down the hall of the PICU, Haley and Darcy in tow. We waved to the nurses and staff as if we were the first float of the Macy's Day Parade gliding down the hallway to the exit. It was nothing less than a magical gift from God, this procession to the doors. I felt like a long jail sentence had finally ended.

We exited the hospital doors and Gracie took her first breath of open air. A person to my left coughed and the person behind her lit a cigarette. We walked a few feet as construction workers drilled and pounded around us, working hard on UVA's beautification project. We came to a busy intersection and I frantically looked both ways, tugging on Colby's arm to be careful. I marveled that the doctors had let us take her out into this environment.

Haley and Darcy loaded up in the car, this time with a little sister in between their car seats. They were full of coos and immediately started talking in a baby voice to her. I could hardly believe that she was with us, and that we got to keep her.

We arrived at the mission house and video taped her whole dramatic entrance, even though she was dead asleep. The night before, Haley had asked me a very logical question. "Mom, when we bring Gracie to this house tomorrow should I say, 'Welcome home?' You know...since this isn't our home?"

For a moment I felt bad for my kids who weren't sure what they could call home, but it ended up being a springboard into a great discussion about the concept of home, and how we will never truly feel at home on this earth. After our conversation, I had made a sign that read, "Welcome Home, Gracie. Home is wherever we are together." That afternoon I sat her in front of it for a picture.

It was such a magical day together. Haley held her for the first time and we looked like the paparazzi trying to capture it all. Darcy put on her swimsuit and walked down the street to the church's garden sprinkler where she was able to unleash her joy. Haley got out her sketchbook and hummed to herself as she drew. Colby took a nap. I tried to take pictures of every moment before it slipped through my fingers. Everyone was just drinking in the sacredness and the gratitude each in their own way.

Colby & Annie,

I'll get a check out this afternoon.
You all continue to be in my prayers. I can't wait for God to reveal the extraordinary things planned for your girl. If there's anything I can do or specifically pray for or whatever, please don't hesitate to ask.

Noel

P.S. If you ever get down to Texas, hit me up for tickets to a Texas A&M Football game. Football's not for everyone, but a game at Kyle Field is an experience.

Noel,
Annie here...I just wanted to say thank you again. You have really no idea how much this has already been a blessing. I just ordered home-school curriculum for the year and it was really nice to do it knowing we had some extra means. I have been thanking God a lot for you lately and praying for spiritual blessings to come your way as you've sent them our way.

Annie,
I'm so glad that I have the chance to help give y'all some breathing room (so to speak). And my grandmother would be ecstatic that she's helping with school. She spent 34 years teaching.
Noel

September was just as hot as August, but worse because the pools were closed.

We stayed at the mission house for a couple of weeks so that we were close to the hospital in case anything happened. Taking care of Gracie was not too difficult. Every morning and evening, Colby would test her oxygen levels by taping her toe to a pulse-ox machine. She had to be given a quarter of a baby aspirin and some lasix to help her body drain the extra fluid. The whole routine was only fifteen minutes out of our day, and to be honest, Colby did it all. I just watched, thankful for a husband who was carrying the weight of so many things.

We brought Gracie with us everywhere...to watch the sunset on top of the mountains, on family walks, and even to Lynchburg to show our children where we met. We were an active family and it felt comfortable to just bring her along wherever we went. This was mostly because our pediatric cardiologist, Dr. Dan was so calm and reasonable and convinced us to treat her like a normal baby (*God Bless You, Dr. Dan*).

In Mid-September, we moved back to the home (that was not really our home) west of Fredericksburg. Pastor Bill and Cindy had graciously let us come back and live in their lake house while we continued the job hunt. One afternoon we set up a sprinkler for the kids to enjoy in the front yard and I put Gracie in her cutest outfit, a brown onesie with hundreds of colorful hearts sprinkled over it. She sat peacefully in her pink bouncy seat, and barely opened her eyes even when I fed her. The kids were having a blast outside, and I walked inside where I heard Colby calling my name.

I came into the room where he was working and saw that he had a hollow look on his face. "What's wrong?" I asked. I knew it was something bad.

"Baby Darryl just passed away."

I closed my eyes as I felt the impact.

I just shook my head and took a deep, long sigh as I tried to imagine the emotions they were feeling.

"I told them we'd pray for them."

He came beside me on the couch and put his arm around me, both of us looking down at our sleeping Gracie swaddled tight and alive.

Colby prayed and I listened.

Tears just fled and I didn't capture the thoughts that ran rampant: *This isn't fair.*

Why would such a thought even occur to me? After all, my daughter was doing well. Why couldn't I just be thankful? There were so many conflicting emotions unsettled on the floor of my heart.

It felt almost like someone had thrown me a gourmet dinner party, but as I sat down to enjoy it, I noticed starving people right out my window. They were coiling with hunger... *but there was no way to share.* All I could do was try to eat and be thankful even though the view was making the food taste bitter.

I was grateful that I was spared the tragedy and *mad that I was spared the tragedy while they weren't.* What could I possibly say to them? I felt like I needed to apologize for God...make excuses for Him...or something. A numb confusion paralyzed me for the rest of the day, staring at my gift that I felt guilty for getting.

23

LILY PADS

"And my God will supply every need of yours accord-
ing to His riches in glory in Christ Jesus."

Philippians 4:19

Colby was intense on the job hunt immediately after we were discharged from the hospital. The pressure began to build...soon we would be transitioning off of the mission board's insurance and Gracie's next surgery was just a few months away. Colby wore the stress well most days, but it was still visible on him like a piece of clothing. It was so easy to forget the bigger picture and get caught up in the anxiety of the moment.

Sometimes, when I tried to act strong and confident, he would try to convince me that *the situation was serious*. I would eventually **believe him** and **panic**, forcing HIM to be the strong one and comfort *me*. Maybe he was just scared that he wouldn't be able to provide for us.

At the end of September, just before the weight cracked us in half, Colby got a part-time job at Pillar Church leading worship. Five years previous, our friends Clint and Jennifer had planted this church in Dumfries, Virginia, which was almost an hour north of where we were living. The part-time job was huge because it allowed us to transition to a reliable insurance at a critical time. I loved the church and just hoped that the hour commute wouldn't be too hard on us and prevent us from being involved.

Going to Pillar Church during this time was like a drink of ice-cold water to a parched throat. I was constantly reminded that His grace was sufficient (2 Corinthians 12:9), that He had called us to hope and a rich inheritance in Jesus (Ephesians 1:18), and that our suffering on earth had value (2 Corinthians 4:17). While there were still things that I didn't understand about God's goodness and justice, I couldn't deny that He was taking care of us. All I had to do was look around…

www.getagarman.blogspot.com
October 23ʳᵈ, 2010

Gold Rain

Right now I (Annie) am sitting under a tree watching a shower of red, orange, and gold rain down all around me. The evening light is catching the leaves at a perfect angle and it illuminates the tree like one grand stainglassed window in this outdoor sanctuary.

We moved again. This is the 8ᵗʰ house we've lived in during the past two years...the adventure continues...

Today finds me in the suburbs of Washington D.C in a subdivision named Montclair, which is very close to Pillar Church. Our friends, Tim and Amanda, are graciously letting us stay at their vacant home while they are in Florida for the next six months. It's unbelievable to me how God is using His body--the local church--to literally hold us during this time of need.

In some ways, I feel like God brought us out of America to bring us back here with new eyes. After spending 15 months in Iceland, I am now enamored with the most mundane, simple things. I just can't stop staring at the trees and vegetation here...every leaf of every plant has a different shape like a mosaic of worshipful green.

I really feel God's eye upon us today. I'm not too worried about the future because I know God has something up His sleeve. Too many things have happened. It's so obvious that God has a plan and I'm learning to just kick up my feet in the passenger seat and trust that the Driver knows where He's going.

The more I travel through life, the more I'm realizing that God determines our steps. Even our choices somehow fit into His mastermind puzzle that we can't even begin to figure out. **So, we don't. We just submit, trust....and then REST.**

Every day we watched Gracie grow. I often stared at her, reminded of how the Bible refers to us as dust (Ps. 103:14). She was like my little dust ball...so delicate and small. Every single moment, I had a tangible reminder of how fragile life was. There were so many things that could go wrong inside of her. The only thing sustaining her life was a tiny shunt that was temporarily being used to direct blood to her lung.

Since Colby didn't have a full-time job yet, that meant we weren't receiving any income. This would have been an impossible situation had it not been for Noel Devin, *who we were beginning to call our Texas angel.* Noel consistently sent us the money she had promised which we were using for food, gas and medical bills.

Whenever I began to take my eyes off of Jesus and panic, He would remind me of this crazy scenario He had orchestrated. It was so humbling to think of God hearing our desperate prayers and responding through Noel's obedience. It was humbling to receive something that was completely undeserved from this stranger who was slowly becoming a friend.

Noel,
Colby here. We just want you to know how much your
kindness has meant to us over the past month or so

since Gracie's birth. As you can imagine the whole event has had its difficult and exhausting moments, **but there have been many times where we have felt like your gift allowed us to make decisions that eased the burden.** *As we have been making decisions and preparing for the transition by looking for a new place of ministry, I am thankful that we have a constant reminder of how God can provide literally out of the blue.* **You have been a part of God's plan to make this a season of life that we will look back upon and rejoice in as we welcomed Gracie into our lives.**

Grateful,

Colby, Annie, and the Girls

Hey there my favorite Texan!

I know Colby wrote you a few weeks ago, but I wanted to take some time to write you myself also. I just wanted to tell you again that you are very much appreciated. There have been MANY times in the last several weeks that something has happened to us and the least stressful solution involves spending money. In the past this would have really stressed me out, but lately Colby has been saying to me, **"Two words...I have two words for you: Noel. Devin."** *I just wanted to tell you that today. I don't know much about you at all, but I know*

that you are sensitive to God's Spirit and for that
we are thankful.
Love from VA,
Annie

~

Annie,
Oh, my goodness. This cracked me up. Most of the
time those 'two words' evoke a different response!

I absolutely love the faces the girls are making in the
latest post. You have a ton of personality on your
hands!
ND

~

The autumn passed quickly and Gracie's life was continuing to be sustained. She stayed healthy all winter, which was kind of shocking since our family had a sticky history of catching whatever was flying around. Our friends would invite us over and our first question would be, *"Is anyone sick?"* followed by, *"Has anyone been sick?"* If people came over to our house, they had to first pass through something akin to TSA security measures complete with antibacterial gel and interrogations.

Although Colby was only part-time, he worked full-time hours to help the church and I began to feel the weight of having three kids and homeschooling two of them. There were so many questions that raced around in my head, never seeming to take a rest: *Where would Colby get a full-time job? Where would that take us? Where would Gracie have her next surgery? Would she make it through? Could God be trusted regardless?* Her second surgery was scheduled for January 17th, 2011.

All we could do was take it one moment at a time. Almost like stepping from one lily pad to another, unsure when the next one would surface, but trusting that it would. After all, many lily pads had surprisingly emerged in the murky waters...a job, two temporary free homes, money from a Texas angel...*we had a lot to be thankful for.*

As the months went on and winter forced indoor activities, I started to feel a strong pull to write and record our journey with Gracie. Writing had always been something that helped me work out my feelings, and I felt like recording everything we'd been through could benefit others in a similar situation. After all, I had already admitted to the blogosphere that I was going to do it. I hated when people said they were going to do something but never followed through. I was stuck. *I couldn't commit my own pet peeve.*

Every week, my friend, Eileen, who was a cancer survivor, let me come to her quiet house to write. So much of the story was in my bones and it wasn't sitting well in there; it needed to be released and recorded and shared. Week after week, in Eileen's guest room, I pounded away at my laptop reliving the events of 2010. Most of those times involved a good crying session as all the emotions bubbled to the surface where I had to face them again. I hated it and loved it all at the same time.

24

BLEACHED WHITE

"There is no fear in love, but perfect love casts out fear."

I John 4:18

I sat down on the nearest thing I could find after reading the message. Although Noel was a new friend in my life, one that I had never even met, the news still felt weighty. **Out of everyone this could happen to, *Noel didn't deserve this.*** I couldn't help but feel it again...this feeling that *life just wasn't fair*...was this the thanks she received? I knew my thoughts weren't right, but I wondered them anyway.

After a few moments of numbness, I read the message again.

Annie and Colby,

My oldest brother was killed in a car accident yes-
terday. He was an extraordinary man. Would y'all
please pray for my family. Nickless and I have two kid
brothers (19 & 17) who are distraught. We're all very
close - to the point we've never quite known where we
stop and the others start. I have always found myself
less whole when we're apart and this is especially the
case today.

I hope you all are well. I would be grateful for your
prayers for Nelson and Neil.
Noel

Why would God allow Noel to go through this? Why would He take
away her brother and friend? Everything human and fleshly
in me cried out that this wasn't fair. It wasn't what she
deserved.

I sighed as I tried to find truth while lies screamed around
me.

Does God really operate this way? Does He withhold things from us
that we deserve? Is this kind of a God really good?

I showed Colby the message from Noel and we both felt
somber the rest of the day. God's ways were definitely mysterious and past finding out. Was I just supposed to accept that?
I was beginning to think that was the only choice.

Noel,
We will definitely be lifting you up. I am so sorry
that this happened and that you lost a brother and

a friend. I wish I had the right words to share right
now; I will be praying for you to trust our good God
during this trial.
Just got your check.
Love to you,
annie

December 2010
9:36 AM.

Breakfast was still scattered across the kitchen table and Gracie
was crying, needing attention. I sighed. School was supposed
to have started almost an hour ago, and having spent three
years as a teacher at an elementary school, I was not used to
such an unstructured environment.

We were still living in our friend's home in Northern
Virginia awaiting a full-time job. Surgery number two was less
than a month away. Even though I didn't think I was nervous,
my body was reacting otherwise. This surgery was going to be
different. Five months had gone by. Five months of being with
Gracie endlessly and developing a special bond.

Now we loved her so dearly and couldn't imagine life without her. I would contemplate these things and eventually feel
one side of my face go numb. I had never experienced anything like it before...*then again, the stress had never been so great.*

"Haley and Darcy, it's time to get dressed. School will be
starting in ten minutes," I felt the blood pressure rising as I
tried to rock the baby while simultaneously wiping down the
counters. *Maybe I should just take the next few weeks off of school,*

I thought to myself as I went to change a dirty diaper. More voices started to compete for the attention: *That is unheard of. We have so much to do; we can't get behind...That would be so lazy.*

I put Gracie in a bouncy seat while I started to teach a Math lesson on the additive property to Haley. I checked to make sure the Moby wrap (one long piece of cloth) was put away because just the day before Darcy had tied her foot to one end of it and attempted to bungee jump off the top of the stairs.

Haley seemed bored and unfocused and I could feel anger starting to simmer. I gave her a worksheet on contractions to satisfy our Language Arts time and tried to pump a bottle for Gracie. I was exhausted by the intense pace that I put on myself and my fears were only adding more weight to the heaviness I carried around. I attempted to correct Haley's worksheet that was full of mistakes.

"Haley Jane," I could hear my tone slipping. "Did you try your best on this worksheet? You did not get a *single* answer right."

I started to go over each answer with her, but her disinterest made my blood hot. I started to get louder with each question. "DIDN'T. See? It's the short way of saying DID NOT. Are you paying attention?" She was looking out the window, looking rather unengaged.

I was starting to lose it.

"Weren't... were not.

Wouldn't... WOULD NOT.

Are you *listening*? I *don't* want to have to go over this **again**!"

My volume was now unnecessarily loud with this child who couldn't quite understand the apostrophe's role in a contraction. The baby was crying in the background and I went upstairs to the bathroom where I tried to get myself together. I watched the water spiral down the toilet and couldn't help but relate a tiny bit.

The next day as I was getting for another doctor's appointment at UVA, I hit an all-time low. Small tasks were overwhelming to me. I was completely paralyzed by how much there was to do, but not sure what to do next and unable to do any of it.

I had been having trouble sleeping at night. I kept envisioning sitting in a waiting room bleached white with fear. I kept imagining the surgeon walking in solemnly and apologetically with the worst news a parent could hear.

I thought that I was doing myself a favor preparing myself for this scene. Almost as if...*if it **did** happen, I would be **ready** because I had already practiced my response.*

Colby (ever the analyzer) told me that I was doing this in an attempt to control my environment. He was probably right. However, I began to realize, in my attempt to control the future and prepare myself for the worst, *I didn't take away any of my stress...*I only added to it.

Before I left for the appointment in Charlottesville, I called my friend Eileen. She was a strong woman and I knew that she would have words for me. After listening to me for a long time, she spoke with understanding. Her advice was simple. "Okay...well, if you must...*Go there...*Go there in your mind."

I shifted uncomfortably as I listened to her. *Maybe I shouldn't have reached out for help,* I thought...I didn't like her cognitive exercise.

She continued. "Go to the waiting room and watch the doctor walk in with his head down. **Imagine** that you are sitting there and your **biggest fear happens**."

I closed my eyes and felt the tepid tears run down my face as I envisioned my worst nightmare coming true.

"Now picture *Jesus* there in the waiting room WITH you, holding you while you get the news..."

I stopped.

There it was.

Jesus.

He had been missing from all of my fantasies and fears. When I envisioned the future and all its uncertainties that were crippling me, I had left the ONE thing out **that mattered the most**.

Despite what happened, Jesus would be there at my side. *Despite what happened, **it would be okay***. It would be okay because it wasn't the end of the story. Death is not the end of the story for believers in Christ.

It was the same lesson I had learned during Gracie's first surgery, but apparently hadn't really gotten down.

Kind of like Haley's lesson on contractions.

God is obviously more patient when He has to repeat Himself.

25

RUBBLE

"The Almighty-we cannot find Him. He is great in power; justice and abundant righteousness he will not violate."

Job 37:23

Getagarman.blogspot.com
January 16th, 2011

The Glenn

That's the name of the surgery Gracie is having to-morrow morning. For the curious reader, you can go check it out online. For the rest of you, it will suffice to say that it is a 4-5 hour open-heart surgical procedure that will help Gracie maintain a tolerable oxygen sat-uration in her blood for the next couple of years. If all

goes well, we should be looking at a 4-6 day stay at
UVA Hospital in Charlottesville, VA. Stay tuned for
updates throughout the day and thank you for your
support and prayers.

≈≈

January 17th, 2011
Charlottesville, VA

Anticipating surgery day was a lot worse than the actual surgery day. I think that's exactly what I said about surgery number one.

Our closest friends came to support us for surgery number two and the waiting room was packed full of support and love. They brought with them such a light, jovial atmosphere that I even remember laughing at one point, despite the seriousness of what was happening right down the hallway in the Operating Room.

I worked on my digital scrapbook. We ate pizza. I told them about my dream to open a Bible museum in Washington D.C. near the Smithsonian museums. I told them about the book I was starting to write and suddenly felt embarrassed because of all the dreams I was juggling.

The surgeon called while we were all in the cafeteria to report that things went smoothly. The time had flown and I couldn't believe that it was over so quick. The whole experience reminded me of a child who screamed and cried for hours because they knew they were going to the doctor's office to get a shot...*only for the actual shot to be done in a matter of seconds.*

I was reminded why the Bible told us not to worry about tomorrow...*we really have no idea what it's going to bring.*

Over the next couple of days, Gracie looked horrible, but I was told that she was recovering just like she should. Because her surgery involved attaching the superior vena cava to her pulmonary artery, she needed to sit up during recovery to ensure proper draining. She looked so uncomfortable and when she cried, I cried. *Is there anything harder than seeing your child in pain and not being able to do anything about it?*

The times that she became ballistic, I felt so emotional and helpless that I would leave her room. Even though I felt like a horrible mother, I wasn't convinced that my presence in her room was really helping during those times. I figured the nurses knew what they were doing, and I tried to get out of the way. When she settled down, I would return to her side. I hated that I was such a lightweight.

Annie's Journal
January 19th, 2011

Gracie is doing great. It's going as perfectly as it could go. On the other side of the room, however, Gracie's roommate is fighting for her life. Parents, grandparents, aunts, uncles, and cousins are standing in the hallway crying, watching as the nurses do a procedure on her limp and nearly lifeless body.

Colby left, but I'm in the room on the other side of the curtain.

The father is weeping as he stands over his baby girl, "You're gonna get better...you hear me?" He's trying to reason with her. "Soon you're going to be all better and we're gonna take you home to your butterfly room."

It's painful to hear him make promises that he most assuredly can't keep.

I try to avoid eye contact with the mother. My baby girl is on the road to recovery and her baby girl isn't. God has answered my prayers for my child to live with a yes and this mother's with a no.

What do you say to that?

I feel like I have to apologize to her for God's decision. Even though I'm on the better end of the deal, I still wrestle with the horror of what is taking place on the other side of the thin curtain. Why me and not her? Why am I spared the trauma that I'm seeing unfold before my eyes?

I closed my computer and stepped out of the PICU to breathe for a little bit. Right outside the doors, a couple was sitting on the floor crying and holding each other. I considered whether or not I should offer to pray with them, but then decided not to interrupt their private time of grieving.

Instead, I stepped inside the waiting room to try to escape. Inside, there was a group of people who I had met the previous day, planning a funeral for their nephew who had just died in a car accident. Beside them sat more family members of Gracie's roommate looking numb and far away. I walked back to our room to find Colby reading from his kindle, looking peaceful.

"Wow, this is a really intense place." I said as I pushed a chair over to him.

"You're so crazy...why did you stay in here during the roommate's procedure ...but have to *leave* every time Gracie cries?" he asked.

"I don't know... I guess when it's *my* baby, I can't handle it. It's so hard to see Gracie in pain and I don't know what I can do to help. I figure the nurses know what they're doing, so I kind of want to get out of the way..."

Colby proceeded to talk to me about circles of responsibility and not getting emotionally involved in other people's drama to the detriment of taking care of my own responsibilities. I understood what he meant, but it felt impossible to emotionally detach when on the other side of the room, a baby girl was slowly slipping away.

I stood up, walked over to Gracie's box where she lay sleeping and prayed that I would be able to be there for her, *whatever that meant.*

 ⤴

On my drive home through the January rain, I tried to get to the bottom of the apparent unfairness. *Maybe it's not God's fault. Maybe I shouldn't be so quick to blame Him.* After a few miles thinking along these lines, a new thought blindsided me. *Maybe the mom did drugs when she was pregnant.* Now it all made perfect sense to me. This was really the mom's fault for being reckless and irresponsible.

I started to feel better as I attributed my daughter's health to my superior pre-natal and post-natal care. The road was curvy and icy, but I started to feel lighter. *God's not to blame... she is.*

My thought was loud enough and vile enough to alarm me.

I had spent the fall reading the book of Job from the Bible and was suddenly struck by how much I sounded like one of Job's judgmental friends. *"These trials are all your fault, Job. You're going through this because you sinned."*

I recalled how, in the first chapter of the book of Job, the audience was given a significant piece of information that Job's friends weren't given. The readers of this book were privy to a scene where God permits Satan to mess with Job and bring excruciating trials into his life. Job's friends, however, didn't know this and were quick to condemn him wrongfully.

I pulled into the driveway and rested my head on the steering wheel as I repented of my wicked heart that was criticizing this mother, condemning God, and searching so desperately for an answer. *I don't know why you're doing this, God. I don't get it. I just **really** don't get you.*

Now, let's just pause the story for one moment. Yes, I realize that I'm supposed to be just letting you watch this scene and perhaps shouldn't interrupt you. But, if I could go into a time machine back to this moment, I would. After first dressing up like a fairy godmother (to really throw myself off), I would enter the car and remind myself ever so gently of some important truths. I would remind myself the rest of the story...of Job who finally, after thirty-seven chapters, hears from God.

"Where were you when I laid the foundation of the earth? Tell me, if you have understanding. Who determined its measurements—surely you know!" (Oh, and I would make myself tell the implied answer which is, *No, I actually don't know.*)

"Have you commanded the morning since your days began and caused the dawn to know its place?" (Job 38:12). "Will you condemn me that you may be in the right? Have you an arm like God and can you thunder with a voice like His?" (Job 40: 8,9). (Answer: "No. No. Nope.")

Just like Job's friends were missing a significant piece of information, so are we, I would remind myself. *God has all the information, sees how it all works together, and asks us to simply trust Him as we stumble through our stories, unaware of the things that only He sees.*

But I didn't have my future self from a time machine or a fairy godmother. I just had my immaturity, my failed memory, my brokenness, my pride, and my feeble attempt at repentance.

I had forgotten, or maybe I had never truly learned, these important truths. The torrential rain pounded on top of the car and I marveled at how quickly I could forget...*If only the storms weren't so good at washing the truth away from our minds... If only truth were tattooed water-resistant on our souls...*

I woke up the next morning after sleeping nine hours through the night. *Why do I feel as though I haven't slept at all?* I just wanted to sleep all day, but as I lay in bed it was clear that my body wouldn't fall back asleep. Every part of me was heavy and I felt like one of the contestants on Biggest Loser who could barely walk up to the scale. Little things, like washing a few dishes and getting myself ready, felt colossal and overwhelming. *Maybe this is just how my body is affected by stress,* I thought, as I got dressed for the day.

We were fortunate to be able to stay at the mission house again for this surgery. It allowed for a good night sleep and a break from the intensity of the Pediatric Intensive Care Unit. The morning sky was clean and outside my window I noticed a magnolia bush that seemed to be bowing in worship. I grabbed my camera and tried to capture the light bouncing off its dew.

I kept walking down the street, slowly and purposefully, hunting for other pieces of beauty in this otherwise brutal and hostile world. I thought about Gracie's roommate, but quickly blinked back the tears and widened my eyes as I looked around me for another photo opportunity.

I guess that's it...that's just what you have to do. I began to reason with myself.

You can choose to stay trapped under the rubble, or you can fight to emerge.

You can choose to hate God and His decisions or you can accept them because you don't know the bigger story line.

You can spit in His face in ignorance or you can bow before Him in gratitude for all the gifts He does give.

I went inside and grabbed a pen and my journal.

Because He does give gifts, you know.

Just look around.

If you search for them, you'll find them...Just like if you seek **Him** *you will find* **Him***...If you search for Him with all of your heart (Jeremiah 29:13).*

I scribbled down my new thoughts, continuing to think about the apparent unfairness swirling all around. *If we all got what we deserved in life, we would be in trouble. We've all sinned in many ways and deserve to pay for it. But, grace is getting something we don't deserve. None of us deserve God's unconditional love and the salvation He offers through Jesus. None of us deserve grace.*

My little Gracie was given to me from the gift giver. *Isn't it up to God what He chooses to give and to whom?* Who was I to judge God? Did I really think I knew more than Him?

I drove to the hospital, ready to humble myself before my God...despite what He decided to give or take away.

26

BRAINSTORM

"For it has been granted to you that for the sake of Christ you should not only believe in him but also suffer for his sake."

Philippians 1:29

Gracie recovered very quickly from her second surgery and we were home in less than a week. She was so resilient; it was hard to believe that she had actually been through a major open-heart surgery. Except for the huge bandage on her chest, there wasn't much evidence.

It was a good thing that Gracie's health didn't provide much drama for the spring of 2011. There was enough to go around as Colby waited for a full-time job.

Money was starting to run out. Tim and Amanda, who were letting us live in their house, were moving back, and we didn't know where or how we would live next. On top of it all, my Dad was having exploratory surgery to determine if a mass entangling his thyroid was cancerous.

It all seemed rather bleak. On my good days, I tried to focus on the facts rather than the feelings (a good lesson learned on the seventh floor). The facts were this: God saw it all. Even stronger...*God had written it all, hadn't He?* Had he brought us back to the States merely to make us homeless and humble us? *Perhaps*...but maybe He had other plans, too. We just had to trust Him while we waited for Him to reveal the next step.

Some days I did this well. Other days, *not so much...*

On one of the hardest days of our wait, I drove to Prince William Forest Park to go running by myself. Halfway down the trail, however, I realized that I was too mentally, physically, and emotionally depleted to finish the run. Colby and I had been fighting more than we ever had. We were both so worn down and hypersensitive, communication and decision-making felt impossible. It was like we were being forced to stand and function while the ground underneath us shook with constant uncertainty.

I curled up in the fetal position in a pile of leaves next to a tree and just sobbed for what felt like hours. "God, do you SEE US?" I screamed to the sky. "What are you DOING to us?" Whatever He was trying to teach me, I clearly wasn't getting.

James 1:2 said, "Count it all joy, my brothers, when you meet trials of various kinds, for you know that the **testing** of your faith produces steadfastness. And let steadfastness have its full effect, that you may be perfect and complete, lacking in nothing." If this was a test, surely I was failing.

After moving out of Tim and Amanda's house, we drove up to Pennsylvania where we stayed with various Garmans for the week. They were all so generous, and hospitable, and I felt lucky to be a part of such a great family. Because we were sleeping in so many different places, Gracie had a tough time sleeping during our trip.

One particular night while Gracie was crying well into the night, I can remember whimpering to myself, "I just want to go HOME!" A few seconds later, I was struck with the harsh reality:

We did not have a home.

The drive back to Northern Virginia from Pennsylvania was awful. Traffic was horrible, it was raining, the kids were fighting, Gracie was strapped in her car seat crying, and Colby and I were arguing about everything. Looking back, I should have shut my mouth and told Colby that I would support whatever decision he thought was best. This would have been the wisest course of action. Unfortunately, I had strong opinions. And I didn't trust him. And thought I knew better than him. And...ahem...*I think you get the picture...*

Pastor Bill knew about our situation and graciously offered to let us live in his house again. His renters weren't moving in for another month, so that bought us a little more time.

We stopped at Pillar Church for a meeting before heading to the Bill and Cindy's house. As I opened the car door, trash and toys and books and bottles fell out onto the ground and I let out a loud and frustrated exhale. This disorganized chaos in our car was just a picture of our lives and on this particular day I was just sick of it.

The pastor of Pillar, Clint, was standing there and I didn't even try to hide my emotions. "Well, that was the worst trip of my entire life," I said to him while I stepped out of the car. He was used to my transparency and he just laughed out loud.

Colby had mentioned that we were going to a meeting at church, but I didn't exactly know what it was about nor did I have energy to care. I fed Gracie who instantaneously became happy again and set the kids up with toys to play with in the nursery. Across the hall, Clint and Colby and some others were sitting in front of a huge dry erase board. I stepped into the room where an intense discussion was going on.

Conversations had begun about a strategy to plant a number of churches near Marine Corps bases and network them together. Our church was only two miles away from the Quantico Marine Corps base, so it seemed like a good idea.

But Pillar was a small church, only seventy members... *and half of those members were children.* Was it possible for such a small church to do such a big thing?

Clint had proposed the idea of making a video to promote the project. The meeting was a brainstorming session about the content of the video. For a couple of hours we talked about the natural movement of the Marine Corps and how that could advance of the gospel. We talked, we drew, we ideated...and I left the meeting that night humbled, my perspective widened beyond my little world.

We moved a few weeks later into an apartment south of the church in Stafford. Haley and Darcy thought we lived at a hotel because it was so small and it had a pool. It was so good to have them around...so upbeat, so excitable, so naïve. Their joy was contagious and we really did have a lot to be thankful for. It had been borderline miraculous that we had lived in the States for a year without having to pay for housing.

But still, the haze of our lives was confusing to walk through. The only way I functioned on most days was by picturing Jesus walking through the haze with me, holding my hand and leading me in a trust walk.

There are multiple journal entries that I could include here to let you in on my roller-coaster emotions during this time. But, perhaps by now *you're sick of hearing about me crying in the fetal position in various places*...so I'll include one of my more positive journal entries.

Annie's Journal
June 1, 2011

We are going to make it.
Step by step.
This next move won't kill us...it will make us stronger...
I need to let Colby lead...and just follow.

We are done panicking.

*Yes, it feels like an army is rushing towards us with spears and arrows...but **I will not fear. What can man do to me? (Hebrews 13:6).***

*I'm ready to **Stand still and see the salvation of the Lord (Exodus 14:13).***

Excited actually.

HOW IS THE LORD GOING TO PULL THIS ONE OFF?

I'm just so curious!

27

THE PLUNGE

*"Whatever the LORD pleases, He does, In heaven
and in earth, in the seas and in all deeps."*

Psalms 135:6

June 24th, 2011
South of Stafford, VA

The windows were down and the wind whipped through
my hair as we drove down I-95. We had gotten a baby-
sitter and were on our way to Virginia Beach for a few
days alone. Colby turned up Chicago's Greatest Hits, letting it
spill out onto the interstate.

A few weeks earlier Colby had come home with some news:
*the elders at Pillar had offered him a full-time job as the teaching pas-
tor at Pillar.*

Was this what God had been preparing for us? It was hard
to know...the job seemed to be a good fit for both of our gifts.
Colby loved to preach, and I loved the missional focus of the

church. If Colby took the position, Clint would be able to focus on training the church planters we had sent out near the various Marine Corps bases.

Pillar was a new church, which in many ways, meant it was a blank slate. We had the opportunity to make Pillar everything we ever dreamed a church could be. *But, there was only one catch.* The church was still small and really couldn't afford to take Colby on full-time.

If we said yes, it would be an act of total faith...or total stupidity. Taking the low-paying job would feel like stepping out of a boat, trusting that either we would walk on water *or die a tragic death, continually reminding society to never step out of a boat again.*

We decided to go away for a few days to process the decision.

After checking in to our cheap motel, we sat on old beach chairs and listened to the hypnotic rhythm of the waves. There was something calming about them as I watched their pace and meditated on the sovereignty of God. Whatever we decided, God would work it out for good. We had weighed all the pros and cons. We had prayed. We had fasted. We had sought counsel. We had really done all we could.

The sun was starting to lower itself behind us and we knew we had to make a decision before it lied down for the night.

Colby and I were lying down on our blanket, facing each other when he said, "Sometimes you just have to take the plunge, right?"

I opened my eyes to look at him even though the angle of the sun was blinding me. It sounded like he was leaning towards a resolution.

"But, it's never easy to take a plunge is it?" He continued.

"No, it isn't…" I knew exactly what he meant.

The evening felt soft on our skin, almost as if silk had been woven into the air. We both stood up and started walking towards the ocean, an explosion of color and light all around us; and, for a moment it all felt magical…like we were on the edge of something unknown, yet beautiful.

If we took this job, it would feel like stepping out of an airplane and into a free fall. *Would God provide for us financially if we did this? Would God take care of us?*

It was cold, but we started running, hand in hand, jumping over the waves until we were past the break. *Hadn't God answered that question enough in the past year…Hadn't we learned anything?*

"Are you ready for this?" Colby looked over at me and I smiled as my response. Together we dove under the cold foamy waters of the Atlantic Ocean, dancing with colors from the sky.

All it took was one quick phone call to Clint to let him know that our answer to his offer was a yes. The next day, Colby began his full-time position as the teaching pastor at Pillar Church and we were so thankful. We decided to continue homeschooling the kids because we would begin house hunting and moving again soon. It felt nice to know what we were doing and have a plan.

One particular afternoon while I was taking a power-nap, I woke up suddenly thinking about Noel Devin. We had stayed in touch throughout the year and, despite the fact that she was dealing with her own grief, she had been a huge support to us through Gracie's surgeries. I woke up overwhelmed by her generosity all over again and wanted her to know it.

I sat down at my computer and typed out our story for Noel, starting at the very beginning. I shared how Colby and I met and how we came to be missionaries in Iceland. I explained the extent of how God used her to sustain us as we waited on a full-time job just in case she hadn't understood. I then shared the recent news of the full-time job at Pillar Church.

If it hadn't been for Noel's gift, who knows what would have happened to us while we waited? My words felt small expressing gratitude for something so big. God had used her to bring us to where He wanted us. How could we ever say thank you?

Not long after sending Noel the message, I heard back from her:

> *Annie,*
> *I've been on vacation and wanted to respond, but doing it on my phone was too complicated. Thank you. That's pretty profound, huh? It's so encouraging that you can see the purpose in our random acquaintance. If I've learned anything in the last eight months, **it's that God really does have a plan and things happen when they're supposed to happen.** I don't know that I ever really considered that before.*
>
> *It's always good to hear from the Garmans! So glad that y'all landed where you're supposed to be.*

Y'all continue to be in my prayers.
Noel

Gracie took her first steps the day that we moved. Our friends were renting out their townhome closer to church, and we decided to move there while we looked for a home to buy. Life was spinning so fast, it just kind of happened in the background. Our heart baby was starting to talk, discover the world around her, and explore her surroundings.

Our lives were so full of church life, house hunting, and homeschooling that I sometimes forgot our baby had a heart defect. She looked and acted completely normal; the only thing we did differently was give her a half of a baby aspirin each day.

The day that Colby taught her the word "scar" and showed Gracie her scar, I felt like I had to shush him. I'm not sure why. I either wanted to grab the camcorder and capture the conversation in our memories, or I wanted to be in control about how it was talked about.

I hadn't really thought about how or when or in what manner we would communicate to Gracie about her heart, and now here he was, just going for it. *I almost didn't want her to know yet.* I watched the two of them interact, remembering all over again her condition and its implications. *It had been awhile since I had remembered.*

28

BURST

*"For I consider that the sufferings of this present time
are not worth comparing with the glory that is to be
revealed to us."*

Romans 8:18

October 19th, 2011
Dumfries, VA

"Colby, do you hear that?" We had both just gone to
bed after an exhausting day of work and parenting. That particular evening I was worn down
more than usual and was actually falling asleep at our small
group Bible study—something that had never happened
before.

The autumn had been a trying time in our lives. Financially,
it was tighter than ever. Soon after Colby came on staff, many
of the families in our church had to relocate to a different

duty station and our small church was now even smaller. At times we even feared we had made the wrong decision.

I had been waiting all day for bedtime to come. The rain was coming down loud and heavy. It was the kind of cozy night that made you thankful your whole family was safe and together inside.

I heard a faint coughing coming from the girl's room and decided to go in and check on Gracie. All three girls shared a room and I tiptoed in while the princesses slept. Gracie, now fifteen months old, was lying in her bed coughing. As I got closer, I could hear her wheezing.

I picked her up and took her to Colby who was almost asleep.

He sat up immediately, but didn't seem too alarmed. "She probably is just getting a cold," he said calmly. He rocked her for a little bit, then put her back in her crib. We both lay in bed, staring at the ceiling, unable to go back to sleep. We wanted to be cautious, but not overreact. It wasn't clear what the next step was. The rain pounded on the roof and Colby made a phone call to her pediatric cardiologist.

We heard some more coughs. A few minutes later we went to check on her and brought her downstairs. She was struggling, *laboring to breathe*. It was like watching a speeding train in front of me. I couldn't process anything that was happening. Colby was putting his shoes on and frantically asking me for the diaper bag. I felt almost paralyzed as I handed him the bag that I knew didn't have anything inside it. I couldn't even form the words in my mouth to explain this to him. I kissed Gracie and she looked at me with scared, red eyes between her gulps for air.

They were gone before I could even come up with a better plan. Haley and Darcy were dead asleep upstairs and it was almost 1:30AM. I got back in bed, imagining Gracie's scared face and the breathing that was strained. I hated that Colby was driving her to the ER by himself. Why hadn't we called an ambulance? I imagined her in the back seat struggling for oxygen *and Colby unable to do anything but drive.* I tried to call, but there was no answer. It was the loneliest and longest forty minutes.

Lying down wide-awake, I felt as though I had just been shipwrecked and washed up on a rocky shore. Every so often, I would feel a wave of anxiety wash over me and through me almost as palpably as though it were real water. My mouth was dry, but I was too heavy with fatigue to get up and get anything to drink.

I finally got a call from Colby saying that they were both on an ambulance to UVA hospital. The rain seemed to come down harder as I envisioned them making the trip on the wet, curvy roads. They had given her a steroid and her breathing was starting to stabilize.

The next morning I dropped the kids off with our friends and drove to UVA in Charlottesville. Gracie had been diagnosed with croup, was given some oral steroids and was ready to be released from the hospital already.

It was unreal. Just twelve hours previous, it had seemed like she was fighting for her life, but now as the dawn reddened, everything was calm and back to normal. Croup was apparently a common thing for heart babies to experience. No one had ever told me. *Then again, I had never asked or looked.*

I don't know if or when I ever recovered from the exhaustion of that week...

Homeschooling with a toddler who had just learned how to unravel an entire toilet paper roll was wearing me out. Every day I seemed to wake up nervous that we would not be able to accomplish everything I felt like should be accomplished on a normal school day.

Gracie was such a loud, active baby that demanded so much attention. Every morning at breakfast I tried to do a Bible lesson with the girls, but Gracie would scream so loud that Haley and Darcy would cover their ears with frustration. "I can't HEAR you!" I remember Haley yelling to me from across the kitchen table. As a teacher who had come from a long line of teachers, this was not how a classroom was supposed to run.

I felt like I was running on fumes by the time December rolled around. Even though I felt very pressured to homeschool the kids until we bought a house and moved and changed school districts again, I knew that I needed help.

The kid's first day of public school I vacuumed out our car and deep cleaned the house and I could almost feel the cobwebs clearing in my mind as well. It was as though someone was releasing air from a balloon that was about to burst... *only the balloon was my head.* I was so thankful for the amazing teachers and staff at Triangle Elementary School. In one sense I felt like they had saved my sanity.

For the first time since her birth, it would be just Gracie and I during the day. I looked forward to more one-on-one time with her and not having to juggle so much.

I wrote out a game plan for taking time to write each week. I had such a desire to write and record Gracie's story, but there had not been much time at all. Why did I feel so compelled to write it all down? I didn't know. All I knew was that it was like a fire in my bones and I needed to get it out swiftly.

29

BACKSEAT DRIVER

"And Mary said, 'Behold, I am the servant of the Lord; let it be to me according to your word.' And the angel departed from her."

Luke 1:38

January 6th, 2012
Dumfries, VA

I tried to sit up in bed and groaned. *When will this end?* I moaned to the ceiling. The kids had only been in public school for five whole days but had managed to catch a nasty virus that they had shared with me.

I had been sick for weeks, and as I tried to get out of bed, I decided that enough was enough. It was time to go to Urgent Care and get on some antibiotics even though I knew I would be letting my homeopathic friends down. I had been sick for too long. Who knew what kind of vicious bacteria was starting to grow inside of me?

On my way to Urgent Care, I stopped by Rite Aid to get a pregnancy test. I knew that the doctors would ask, and I wanted to be confident so that I could get on the strongest medication possible.

Someone had just gotten sick in the women's bathroom at Rite-Aid and it was closed for cleaning. Thinking it would only take a minute, I locked myself in the men's bathroom to take the test. Every other time I'd done this, I'd shaken with anticipation, but this time I didn't. Within seconds, two lines appeared, declaring loudly that I was pregnant.

I dropped it in the sink as if it was a hot potato. "Darn you, Annie...you're so cheap!" was my very first thought. I had bought the cheapest generic pregnancy test and *the only rational explanation to what I was seeing **was that the test was wrong.***

"This cannot be real. This cannot be real." I looked into the mirror and kept repeating those four words. *I hadn't even slept in the same bed as my husband for over three weeks. How was this physiologically possible? But, besides that...how would we fit another child in our car? In our townhouse? In our budget? In our busy schedule?*

I must have been in the men's bathroom for over twenty minutes. Eventually—after going through every possible emotion – I gathered my wits enough to exit Rite Aid.

It was then time for absolute and total panic.

WE WERE ABOUT TO HAVE ANOTHER BABY...and we hadn't even taken down our Christmas tree yet. It was as though the baby was coming out in the next four hours...

I rushed to the post office, sent my brother his late Christmas present, hurried to the DMV to put my new address on my license, ran home, washed everyone's sheets and bedroom windows, and frantically took down the Christmas tree. I finished my tirade and collapsed on the couch. I felt only slightly more prepared.

When I told Colby the news, his eyebrows rose high and stood there for longer than normal. The very first words out of his mouth were, "I guess we have to buy a mini van."

One by one, I presented to him the reasons we were doomed, and each one he met with, "It will be okay; God will provide." I told him that it felt like an immaculate conception and he told me that it was both naïve and sacrilegious to feel that way. Either way, the pressure was on to buy a house that would fit all of us.

When we told the girls, Haley and Darcy screamed and ran around our narrow townhouse in a fit of hysteria. "Is it a girl? Is it a girl?" Gracie toddled behind them screaming even though she didn't comprehend an ounce of it.

Before the sun set on that wild day, I read through the account of Mary in Luke's gospel. Upon hearing the news of the conception in her womb, she had lifted her hands in surrender to God's plan. I read the Magnificat and made it my prayer of surrender.

The days went on, and before every meal they consumed, Haley and Darcy prayed for a girl. I didn't care. I was just praying for a healthy, four-chambered heart. I knew that the chances of this child having a heart defect were actually greater than they had been with Gracie.

I had recently broken down at our church's prayer meeting, exposing my fears about this pregnancy. One of our elders, Jack Catalano, had prayed specifically and powerfully for me and our new baby. Even after the meeting ended, I know he and many others continued to pray for us.

As the months went on, I felt a peace that was stronger than the panic. A trust greater than the fears. The anxiety that had once gripped me was starting to lose its strength. God's Word was washing away the lies...lies that I was in control and that *I needed something other than God to be okay.*

This was evidenced even more to me in the spring when I went to a pre-natal appointment. My nurse, after looking through my chart and asking some questions, realized that my previous child had a congenital heart defect. For a brief moment, she seemed to step out of her role as a nurse practitioner and into the role of real-live human being.

"Aren't you nervous?" she asked. She knew the risks.

Since she had initiated this conversation that was a little below the surface, I didn't mind diving even deeper.

"I'm actually not..." I responded.

Her eyes searched me as I spoke about God's faithfulness and His provision and how He was teaching me to just trust Him. I listened to the words coming out of my mouth, and I realized that I was crossing a bridge to a new place. A place I had always wondered about, but never been.

More than anything, *I knew that if it happened again, God would see me through.* He would see us through.

He had and He *would...and He was even now.*

At the twenty-week ultrasound, the whole family crowded into the small room. The nervousness was there, but it didn't have control. The anxiety was present, but it was more like an annoying backseat driver. You just had to make a decision not to hand over the keys.

That day, as my husband held my hand, and all three of my girls crowded around the screen, the following comments could be heard floating from our room.

Ultrasound Technician: "It's a girl!"

Annie (whispering to Colby): "I'm sorry...so sorry...."

Colby: "That's absolutely ridiculous. Please stop talking."

Annie: "What are the Chances? WHAT are the CHANCES?! I mean...WHAT. ARE. THE. CHANCES?!"

Colby: "The chances are *one in two.*"

Haley: (Unintelligible remarks interspersed with exuberant screaming)

Gracie: "Loud. Too loud."

Darcy: "I get another sister!"

Ultrasound Technician: "I see a healthy, four chambered heart. How does that sound?"

$\wp$

Writing. I was starting to hate it.

I was paying a friend to watch Gracie one morning a week so I could focus on extracting the words from the wounds, but it was more painful than I had counted on. For the first thirty minutes of each writing session, I had to fight mean voices that told me I was wasting money and using my time unwisely. Some mornings I would just stare at a blank screen, horrified by each minute that passed unproductively.

The pressure was intense, the inner dialogue was like a boxing match, and if someone had peeked in my window they would have witnessed me doing jumping jacks and slapping myself repeatedly as part of my writing warm up. I absolutely *hated* not finishing something I had started, so I was trapped. I either would drive myself nuts finishing it or drive myself nuts *not* finishing it.

Luckily during this time I met a neighbor who happened to be a writer. We sat on the front steps of our townhomes and talked as his cat, Captain Midnight, used our legs as his scratching posts. He told me stories about his writing classes and I took notes, as if trying to squeeze a Literature degree right out of him. One thing he told me made me want to quit right then and there. One day, one of his professors had brought in an entire suitcase full of rejection letters. His advice to his students was, "If you can't take rejection, then you're in the wrong business." Surely I was in the wrong business. Or maybe this was exactly how God wanted to grow me...

30

WINK

"But he said to me, 'My grace is sufficient for you,
for my power is made perfect in weakness.' Therefore
I will boast all the more gladly of my weaknesses, so
that the power of Christ may rest upon me."

2 Corinthians 12:9

Penelope Raine Garman entered our world on September 5th, 2012. Named after her Grandma, Connie Lorraine Garman, she was a delightful surprise to our family. Every day I thanked God for giving me this gift that I hadn't asked for. It was so fun to see the girls love and care for their new baby sister.

Gracie, now two years old, didn't know what to think. She struggled for a few weeks as she came to the realization that she was no longer the baby, but eventually accepted her new role as a big sister. Gracie's health was tremendous and besides occasionally having purple lips, it was easy to forget that she only had half of a heart.

On the last night of 2012, we let our oldest girls stay up late so they could watch the apple drop in New York City. For hours we watched old home videos and it made Haley laugh so hard that she got the hiccups.

I must have been too wound up when I tried to go to sleep, because I lay in bed for a long time unable to relax. I found myself thinking about 2013. Gracie's open-heart surgery loomed over me like a dark, threatening storm cloud. *Would she be okay? Would this be the time that she'd have complications?* Her scar had healed so nicely and it broke my heart to think of it getting cut open again.

Minutes after having this thought, I heard Gracie in her room crying and coughing. I went in and saw her laboring to breathe with tears streaming from her eyes. Feeling lightheaded, I picked her up and brought her into our bedroom.

"She can't breathe, Colby," I said loudly and felt relieved the moment he sat up. He always had such a level head in the midst of stress. I knew in my brain that she was not dying, but all of my senses were telling me otherwise. Her little eyes were so wide with fear as she gulped for air. We brought her outside where the cold winter air seemed to stabilize her breathing.

We had been through this before. We knew it was croup and we just needed to get her on steroids. We wrapped her in some blankets, I played some Jesus songs on my phone for her, and Colby called pediatric cardiology. The cold January air miraculously helped and eventually her breathing normalized enough that we were all able to go back to bed.

When we awoke the next morning to a new year, Colby didn't waste any time taking Gracie to Urgent care. She was given some medicine and immediately started doing better. All day long, however, I felt the weight of 2013 and the serious things that lie ahead.

I knew I couldn't do it alone. I knew I couldn't make it through the year in a way that honored the Lord without His strength and the prayers of His people.

That morning, I knew I had to humble myself and reach out to a group of friends asking for prayer. I opened up my computer and sent a message asking for some specific things: That I would be able to fight the crippling anxiety leading up to this open-heart surgery, that I could be there for Gracie, that her surgery would be free of complications, that our marriage would be strong in the face of stress, and for God to use us to dispense his grace and strength to others at the hospital during this time.

When I was done sending the very vulnerable email, I sat back and reflected on the net of support that was beneath me, a safety net that had been knit by God through His people. It made walking the wire of an open-heart surgery much less scary. Even when you looked down.

Annie's Journal
February 1st, 2013

God is preparing Gracie for what is about to happen to her. I can see it.

Her eyes are brave and her lips are always singing the third verse of a song (rare for a Baptist, let's just be honest). "God helps me. God helps me. In my Bible book it says that God helps me."

Darcy cried on Tuesday night and Gracie consoled her like a mature adult. She calmed Darcy's fears and tears as she kept repeating, "Don't wowry, Cy-Cy. I ok. I be bwave." Gracie's eyes were big and I'm not sure if she knew what she was saying. Surely she couldn't know. Or could she?

Today I'm enjoying the girl's naptime while the wind howls outside, rattling the windows as February tries to let itself in. As I lay still, I envision combing Gracie's golden, strawberry kissed hair the morning of her surgery. I think of how I will have to fix it special since I won't have a chance to do it for many days after. What will I do? Braids? Pig tails? Whatever I chose will have to be tight. Like a hug that she can feel even when I'm not there.

The wind sings a song as I continue to daydream. I imagine seeing her immediately after surgery, hooked up to life-sustaining machines.

In braids.

Oh God, help me…

There are a lot of emotions and we are six months away from the surgery.

On Monday, April 20th we drove to Charlottesville for Gracie's heart catheterization. This procedure was required so that the doctors could prepare for her surgery. We had gone through a heart catheterization before, and with very little drama, so the anxiety before this event was pretty low.

The part that had me most concerned, though, was handing her over to the OR team. In her last two surgeries, I had not been there for the "hand off" because it was too emotional for me to handle. This time, however, I knew that I needed to be there. *Gracie was more aware now.* Ready or not, I was going to do my best.

The anesthesiologists gave her a sedative called Versed to drink and within minutes, it helped her relax. She was acting drunk, giggling and losing control of her actions. We took videos of her putting on a show and when the anesthesiologist came to take her away, she waved a happy, loopy goodbye. Colby and I looked at each other. The handoff was easier than I had feared...almost too easy.

The heart procedure went fine, but when the pain medicine wore off and she started to wake up, it was a completely different story. Terrified. Disoriented. It reminded me of the transformation scene in *The Incredible Hulk*. Nothing seemed to calm her down.

I tried to hold her, but she just kicked and screamed and hit me as she tried to escape. Singing songs or praying over her didn't take any of the terror out of her eyes and I started to worry that she would be traumatized for life. *Would she ever trust us again? How could she?* Thinking about that question made me completely break down.

After having to put an oxygen mask on her (which made things look so scary), her oxygen levels began to normalize. Perhaps the anesthesiologist had warned me about this re-action and I hadn't been listening *(a very real possibility says my ever gracious husband)*. Perhaps not. Either way, I was not prepared in the least for her to regain consciousness and act like a wolverine. She had just been a baby last time she had this procedure, and she had only been fussy and sleepy.

Eventually Gracie started to relax, which allowed us to feel relieved and more relaxed too. We were able to go back to our room after awhile where she laid in bed watching TV and eating saltine crackers the rest of the afternoon. Our nurses reassured us. Gracie wouldn't be traumatized for life or lose trust in our ability to take care of her...*She probably wouldn't even remember it...*

I walked out of our room in the Cardiac Transition Unit and immediately thought of Noel Devin. She had sent me a sweet message during Gracie's last catheterization procedure and I had read it at that very spot outside the door. Noel had been travelling for work and happened to be flying over Virginia that day in 2010. She was praying for us, knowing that 33,000 feet below her Gracie was having a procedure done on her heart that morning. Ironically, at that exact moment, the pilot had announced that they were flying over Charlottesville.

I stood there, smiling, remembering our Texas angel. And remembering that God likes to wink at us sometimes.

ℒ

Hey there Noel!

It's been a long time since I've written you a note. Last night we had some visitors from church (Texas A&M alumni) over for dinner and we got to telling them the story of our adventure that was the last few years. I just wanted to tell you that you were a big part of that story!

We told them how God used you to sustain us financially during a very difficult time, how He used you to give us patience as we waited for a full time job and how ultimately we then were offered the job at Pillar Church. It's pretty crazy to think how God used you...We would not be where we are today if it wasn't for you....and we don't even know you! I just love the body of Christ!

I wanted to say thanks again and just encourage you as you follow Jesus!
Annie

P.S. I would love someday to have you come out here, meet the Pillar family and see how God is working in and through us to plant churches around this area.

31

THE BRIDGE

"And after you have suffered a little while, the God of all grace, who has called you to his eternal glory in Christ, will himself restore, confirm, strengthen, and establish you. To Him be dominion forever and ever. Amen. "

I Peter 5:10

July 8ᵗʰ, 2013
Dumfries, VA

I woke up with a dry mouth and a nervous stomach. It was as though fear was pounding on the door, begging to come in. As best as I knew how and through the strength of the Holy Spirit, I made a decision to lock the door. I absolutely refused to think about the next moment. *In this moment, everything is fine,* I had to keep reminding myself. ***And in the next moment, Jesus will be there.***

The next day we were going to UVA for Gracie's final open-heart surgery.

After a morning of packing, Gracie and I had a quiet lunch together. In between nibbles of her egg sandwich she looked up at me with wide, azure eyes. "God gonna be with me," she said.

She looked down at her plate and nodded to herself.

"Yes, Gracie. He is. You are so brave," I responded. There was really not much left to say.

The previous Sunday at church, the entire congregation had gathered around our family and prayed for us. For some reason, it felt exciting and that surprised me. I wasn't expecting it to feel that way. Someone, probably Miss Lee or Amanda, prayed and thanked God that Gracie was able to have the surgery so that her heart could be fixed. It was a great perspective and I was ashamed that I had rarely thought to pray that way.

Even though we had just gotten news from the Ronald McDonald house telling us that they were full, and the mission house in Crozet was unavailable, I refused to worry. God would provide. He had proven that enough times and in enough ways.

Sitting there at the table with my two-year-old who was hours from having her chest cut open and her heart stopped, I felt a strength that I hadn't known. I knew it wasn't my own. I could feel the prayers almost physically...lifting me and holding me and squeezing me like a tight embrace.

It's amazing how when things are hard, God blinds you with blessings if you're willing to look up at the Son.

July 9ᵗʰ, 2013
Charlottesville, VA

We arrived at the hospital while the sun was still hiding behind a thin film of stratus clouds. UVA's beautification project appeared to be almost done and we walked into an atrium that was a bright, heaven white. I lifted my head to take in the breadth of the high ceilings and large windows and a particular line from Sunday's sermon kept squeezing my heart. "You make all things new."

I smiled.

The Pre-Op appointment included blood pressure, drawing blood, an EKG, an Echo and an X-ray. "Is this the suwr-gewr-ey?" Gracie asked at one point. We wanted to laugh and cry at the same time.

Later that evening, we drove to Lewis Mountain Road where we would be staying for the week. Colby had contacted the pastor of Charlottesville Community Church earlier that week and told them about our need for housing. Not long after, we got an email from a couple who lived a mile from the hospital. They had extra rooms, and to top it off, they felt they had been given their home so they could be hospitable to others.

When we walked in to our new friend's home, it was like stepping into an HGTV Magazine. I just shook my head and said to God under my breath, "I am not even surprised." We gave Gracie a bath and put her to bed under a yellow and white quilt.

That evening I went for a short run through the UVA campus. The leaves of the magnolia trees looked glossy and magical under the Jeffersonian street lights. If I used my imagination, each limb of the tree looked like it was holding out a bouquet of green. I kept smiling and couldn't understand why I felt so much joy. Everything just felt so new and fresh. The new place to stay. The new hospital. The new heart that Gracie would be experiencing. The new strength that I felt rising.

Annie's Journal
July 11, 2013

Today was Gracie's final open-heart surgery. I slept amazing the night before and had so much peace that it really did pass understanding. Friends from Northern Virginia crammed in the waiting room and prayed for us. I knew I wasn't in control today and this was such a comforting thought.

Everything went as perfectly as it could go today and she was even extubated (breathing tube was removed) right after surgery. Now she is sleeping peacefully, on the road to recovery. I am overwhelmed with prayers and peace.

The steadfast love of the Lord never ceases. His mercies never come to an end. They are new every morning. New every morning. Great is your faithfulness, Oh God. Great is your faithfulness.

Wednesday, July 18th, 2013

"Mommy, can I go to school?" Gracie asked from her hospital bed. The last eight days had been quite the ride with our little (almost) three year old. It had been much harder to watch her recover this time, perhaps because she was older and more aware at times. When she had finally woken up after her surgery, she had gone ballistic and tried to escape from her bed of wires, screaming, **"I want to get out of here...take me with you!"** It had been awful to watch, but I stayed at her side, holding her hand, and assuring her that I wouldn't leave.

"School is closed for the day, baby. The teachers have all gone home," I got in close to her eyes that were fixated on the Teenage Mutant Ninja Turtles on TV. She had loved going to UVA's playschool since she had been released from the PICU and gone to the pediatric wing. It was so good to see her in better spirits. For a few days following her surgery, she hadn't been able to keep any food down. I handed her some graham crackers and watched her scarf them down and ask for more apple juice.

I sat there thinking about our past week. One of the more memorable days of the recovery had been when our friend Becky came for a visit. Gracie was having the stitches on her neck removed, and I was holding her hand watching it all. She was screaming, I was crying, and eventually Becky passed out. Luckily, nurse Jen caught her on the way down and the EMTs didn't have to take her to the ER even though they rushed up to help. When she came to, she apologized profusely. What could we say... *the intensive care unit was a pretty intense place to be.*

Even though this surgery had been the toughest, I sensed that God had toughened me in preparation for it. The happiest day was when she took her first steps around the PICU. We cheered and celebrated as though we had never seen her walk before.

As Gracie and I sipped on another round of Orange Juice, the nurse came in and told us it was probable we could go home the next day. The recovery process had been arduous... I couldn't believe we had made it to the finish line.

On our final evening in the hospital, Colby copied the rough draft of my book onto his kindle and sat back in his chair next to me. A cup of hospital coffee in one hand. Our story in the other. He paused after *Chapter One* and we reminisced of that distant day in 2010 when our lives had turned upside down.

He continued reading, and I continued writing...documenting the final chapter that was unfolding all around me. A couple hours later, I decided to give my brain a break and check my email.

I didn't know the woman real well, but she had heard of Gracie and sent me a message to encourage me. She had promised to pray, but then added, **"I don't know how you do it...I could never handle what you're going through."**

I sat still for a long time after I read that line. After a few quiet minutes, I was finally able to articulate what had struck me.

That was me.

This woman was on the other side of the bridge, looking across with a heart beating to the rhythm of fear. She was wondering what she would do if she was in *my* story.

That *was* me.

I wanted to reach across the bridge from where I stood and grab the hand of this woman. I wanted to look into her eyes, deep into the wondering, and tell her that it would be okay. That she COULD handle it…whatever IT ended up being…not because SHE was strong enough but because God's arms were strong enough.

That there would be surprises of joy around every turn if she pressed hard into Jesus and trusted Him recklessly.

That she would find Him to be enough and more.

Meanwhile, the clocked ticked away in our small hospital room. The pages filled. The chapters turned. And, as each moment passed, the miracle of healing ran deep beneath Gracie's skin.

And then I realized it.

God's answer had not been *no* to our requests for healing after all.

There is something beautiful about beginnings and endings.

Weddings.

Sunsets.

Newborns.

There was something beautiful about the morning on Thursday as I walked from Lewis Mountain Road to the hospital. Maybe it was the ivy climbing on the curvy walls, like little green prisoners trying to escape. Maybe it was the reddish bricks starting to jaundice at the corners, aging so grandly. Maybe it was the Rhododendron and Caladium lining the path to NewComb Hall.

Maybe it was the light of our journey's sunset splashing.

The automatic doors to the hospital opened and I walked through, hitting a wall of both air conditioning and live piano music. There was a ribbon-cutting ceremony going on, celebrating the completion of UVA's renovations. It was almost as if a soundtrack was playing in the background and our story was on the big screen, playing the last scene.

I pressed the button for the elevator and looked down at my feet while I waited. For the first time I noticed a silver lining on the colorful blocks that patterned the floor. For some reason, it made me smile and snap a picture.

On the seventh floor, I walked in as Colby arrived with a kicking and screaming Gracie in his arms. She did not want to leave her hospital playschool. *Like a child content to play in mud puddles, unable to fathom the wonders of the sea.* We tried to reason with her, entice her with the prospect of seeing sisters. She stopped for a moment, starting to remember her life outside the hospital doors.

We packed up our things, I brushed her strawberry curls, and put her in a fresh teal dress that sparkled with silver sequins. We were moments from leaving. Moments from closing the chapter, or ending the story, depending on how one would look at it. Gracie sat in her bed and waited, playing a little in the last rays of our journey's light.

A nurse came in to take off the last of her connections and EKG stickers. I was smiling so wide my cheeks began to cramp as I watched the final wires from her final surgery come off.

There was nothing left to do, so we took a picture of Gracie with her arms wide open, showing the world her wings...smiling as one who had just been set free.

EPILOGUE

"The LORD is good to all, And His mercies are over all His works," (Psalms 145:9)

April 9ᵗʰ, 2014

It was a typical Garman morning. Everyone was rushing around trying to do what they needed to before school started. Gracie, whose oxygen level was now well over ninety percent, ran around the living room with periodic jumps onto the couch. All four girls talked over each other, each trying to get in their word. I saw my phone blinking, alerting me to a new message, and justified that I had time to check it while I went in the bathroom.

New message from Karla Devin.

I didn't know exactly who that was, but recognized the last name.

I quickly skimmed the message sent from a stranger.

Annie,

    I am the mother of Noel Devin. I want to tell you how much she loved your family especially your children. From the moment she learned of your daughter's health, she became her champion spokesman. She loved to talk about your family, the antics of the children, and where everyone needed to pray for each one.

    Thank you and your family for blessing my daughter's life so deeply and abundantly. She loved and cared for each one of you.

In Christ Alone,
Karla Devin

Why was Noel's mother sending me a message like this?

And why was she using *the past tense* to talk about Noel?

A heavy weight began to descend. Colby came into the bathroom and I immediately asked, "What happened to Noel Devin?"

"Nothing, what do you mean? I just heard from her last week."

I followed him to the desk where he googled her name.

Instantly the page filled with links to articles and news stories. Colby clicked and I started to read.

http://www.kbtx.com

Neighbors, Friends React to Deaths of Noel Devin and Her Father Mac

Bryan, Texas:
Neighbors and friends are still reacting with shock to
the news of two Texas A&M former students found
dead after a Bryan House Fire Monday morning.
And now we're learning more about the man police
believe set the home on fire.

Dennis Wayne Brown is in jail for arson, burglary of
a habitation, and unauthorized use of motor vehicle.
His bond is set at more than $1 million.
Thursday we found out from the Texas Department of
Criminal Justice that in a prior 15 year stint in jail
for a robbery, he was denied parole five times.

The fire broke out early Monday in the 2000 block
of Vinewood Drive in Bryan and police say evidence
shows it was started with fuel-soaked rags.
The bodies of 32-year-old Noel Devin, and her fa-
ther, 63-year-old Thomas "Mac" Devin were dis-
covered inside...

We both stood with our hands covering our mouths as the
news downloaded into our minds and hearts. Gracie walked
into our room without asking and started to ask for a drink.
Darcy followed her in and asked if I would get the knot out of
her hair.

There was no time to process the grief and the horror.

I finished pouring cereal and combing hair in a zombie-
like state. The rest of the day passed in a fog, the news heavy
on every single moment.

Later that evening when the kids were all home from school, we sat them down on the couch for story time. We weren't sure how much they knew, so we started from the very beginning. I opened the very first message Noel had ever sent us and read it to them.

They were instantly engaged. It read like a good book, our messages back and forth to each other, and their eyes got big when they found out how much money she had given us. We paused between the messages to explain what had been going on in the background of their little lives at the time. Gracie's open-heart surgeries. Daddy's job search. The economic recession. Through it all, God had used Noel to remind us of His faithfulness and provision.

> Garmans,
>
> Y'all have been such a blessing to me during the last six months. I wish I could explain. I'm so glad that, for once, I followed through when I knew what I was supposed to do.
>
> On my flight this morning, as I stared half-awake out the window thinking about y'all, the pilot announced that Charlottesville was visible. Praying for y'all today. Even at 33,000 feet.
> ☺
> Noel

Haley, our nine-year old, grew skeptical as we continued reading the messages. "Why are you telling us this story right now?" She asked. Her little arms were crossed over her chest and her eyes shifted between mom and dad. "Did something happen?"

I held her hand as I read the last note that I had written to Noel.

Colby shifted around as he began to share the end of the story. *Noel passed away this week,* he told them, and a collective gasp went up from the room.

Darcy wrapped her little arms around my neck and started to whimper, then Haley, and before we knew it, everyone was weeping and holding each other.

I looked up at the ceiling and pictured Noel somewhere above, watching the scene below. I waved and mouthed, 'Thank you,' just in case she could see us. Then I said thank you to Jesus because surely He could see us. He had convinced me of this through Noel.

She was home now. It was hard to believe. Her race was over and none of us could've guessed that she would have crossed her finish line this soon.

Someday we *would* meet...we could hope in this... and it was all because of Jesus.

Because of the timing of the funeral, we weren't able to go. I felt awful and guilty and sad and many other things because I missed it. But, before the year ended, Noel's mother flew out to meet our family and gave us a DVD of the funeral to watch.

At the funeral, Pastor Jonathan spoke through a tight throat. He spoke of Noel and Mac's lives that were marked with generosity and love for others. The room was silent as he spoke of the great injustice that Noel and Mac had experienced. And, from my screen over a thousand miles away, I watched and resonated with every single word that he spoke:

Nine days ago a man broke into the home of my friend Noel Devin and took the life of Noel & Mac.

I'm angry. We hurt for their family. We grieve with them. A great, GREAT injustice took place.

But we know this...Gospel light shines brightest in the darkness, and God will use every bit of this tragedy for the advancement of his kingdom, his glory and the gospel. How do I know this?

God is no stranger to injustice.

At the cross, God used the greatest injustice this world has ever seen to accomplish the greatest good this world has ever known.

This is the gospel. God loves sinners and saves them - at great cost to Himself.

On October 30, 2013, the anniversary of her brother's death, Noel posted this message on her facebook wall:

"Thanks to everyone for the kind words and sweet messages today. It continues, three years later, to astound me how well loved Nickless is – and our whole family for that matter. I know, without a doubt, I'll see him again. And that makes getting through every day without him so much more bearable. **If you don't know that kind of peace, I pray you will.**"

Mac and Noel knew a peace that surpassed understanding. They knew a peace that rose above the earthly trials and pain they had experienced. They knew peace because they knew the Peacemaker. Mac and Noel trusted in the righteousness of Jesus Christ alone as their hope, their life and salvation. They are in the presence of Jesus.

We're here now wrestling with this tragedy, questioning and wondering. The struggle is ours, not theirs. They've seen the face of Christ. They will never taste sin and death again. We wrestle with this injustice, but their struggle is over.

This is why: **At the cross, God used the greatest injustice this world has ever seen to accomplish the greatest good this world has ever known.**

Romans 5:8 tells us, "God demonstrates his love in that while we were yet sinners, Christ died for us."

We don't have to work our way to God. The temple curtain was torn in two from top to bottom signifying God had made a way for man to be made right with him. Jesus was crucified as the perfect substitute for our sin.

Ephesians 2:8-9 says, "For by grace you have been saved through faith. And this is not your own doing;

it is the gift of God, not a result of works so that no one may boast."

And this Sunday, on Easter, we celebrate the truth that Jesus didn't stay in the grave, but he defeated sin, death and the enemy by rising from the dead.

The call is simply this: Believe on Jesus.

*If you're here this afternoon, and you don't know the hope and the peace that the Devins knew, **the call is to believe.** Maybe you've struggled with your own brand of injustice. Maybe your life bears the scars and wounds of wrongs perpetrated against you as well as wounds from your own mistakes and sins.*

You to need to know: You are on the heart and mind of God.

*He loves you. **He doesn't have to do anything else to prove his love. It was proven at the cross.** Believe on Jesus.*

*How do we celebrate the lives of these two people that made such a lasting impact? **Let us worship the God who loves them and has welcomed them into his presence.***

FINAL THOUGHTS

August 2015

I've read the words of this sermon over and over, wishing that they could somehow move through the membrane of a screen into a soul.

Injustice.

Living out this story has forced me to bump up against this word more than once. The truth is, I have hesitated to share our story because I haven't experienced much injustice *compared to some of you.* Maybe some of you read this story and rolled your eyes at the small trial I had to endure compared to yours. Maybe your child has spent hundreds of weeks in the hospital...*maybe you never got to bring your child home...*

I haven't known what to think of that apparent injustice.

I've struggled to understand why my baby lived and someone else's baby did not. I've struggled to justify why some are spared tragedy while others drink of it deeply.

I've struggled long and hard to make sense of it all.

I've fumbled around for over a year, attempting to tie a nice neat bow at the end of this story that has evoked so many questions in my heart...*after all, isn't that what a book is supposed to do?*

I've wrestled and I've searched, and I've come to this conclusion: **The answer to most of the 'why' questions in life can never be answered while we wear these bodies.**

Perhaps I felt it most recently at my friend, Adam's, bedside. He was in his final hours and his closest family and friends gathered around his frail body to sing to him. I held his wife, Chelsea's, hand and looked around the room as we sang about the goodness of God and wondered if anyone else felt the apparent irony. We were circled around his withering body that we had, months previous, laid hands on and pleaded with God to heal.

I thought of how anyone peeking in the windows might be confused. Could this God that we lifted up be worthy of praise *even though the cancer flourished?*

Was God still good? Was He...*really?*

Colby was writing his sermon last night and needed me as a sounding board. The passage was Matthew 7 and we read it together.

> "*Ask and it will be given to you;* **seek, and you will find; knock, and it will be opened to you.** *For everyone who asks receives, and the one who seeks finds, and to the one who knocks it will be opened. Or which one of you, if his son asks him for bread, will give him a stone... If you then, who are evil, know how to give*

good gifts to your children, how much more will your
*Father who is in heaven **give good things** to those who*
ask him!

He had asked for my input, so I felt free to express my true opinion.

"Whatever you say tomorrow, please say it with Chelsea in mind," I reminded him. She was so heavy on my heart. *What would she think of this passage?*

The funeral had just been ten days previous.

"I mean, she asked, she sought, she knocked...she did all those things, pleading for God to miraculously heal Adam," I went on as I lay on our bed. "She begged for **bread**...but it probably feels to her right now that God has given her a **stone**."

"But, THAT'S FAITH." He exclaimed. "Faith is believing that God has **not** ultimately given her a stone, but that He is giving her bread."

I began to sit up, the epiphany hitting me as well. **That was the faith that we were told to have.** Not faith that God would *give us what we asked for,* but **faith** that God would *give us what He deemed best.* Faith that **believes God** when He says it's bread...even though it looks and feels like a stone. Faith that trusts the goodness of God.

I'm not sure why God has taken me on this journey, but perhaps He wanted to humble me and show me the cracks in my own faith. I had always heard that God was good and just, but walking this road made me really stop and ask that question for myself. Not just for me, but for everyone on similar journeys.

Is God really good?

What I've learned is that I can't look to circumstances around me to answer that question.

God is not good just because our daughter is alive. *Please don't misunderstand the message of this entire story.*

If Gracie's health deteriorates, God will still be good.

If God answers our next request with a no, He will still be good.

If tragedy lurks beyond the next corner, God will still be good.

And because He is good, He can be trusted.

As I continue through life, my faith will inevitably be tested by hotter fires. Instead of worrying about this, I have to remember that, *even then, Jesus will be with me,* reminding me of His love, faithfulness, and goodness.

In that day, I pray that my wobbly faith will be found stronger than before.

I pray that I will have learned my lesson well and trust God to carry me over many bridges to deeper places of trust and rest in Him.

"Give thanks to the Lord, for He is good, His faithful love endures forever."

Psalm 136:1

ACKNOWLEDGMENTS

This all started when I heard a really loud idea in my head. The idea (**"You should write all of this down"**) made me stop in my tracks at the top of the stairs the morning of Gracie's first surgery. Almost simultaneously, I heard the voices of many of you who had encouraged me on our blog. Becky, Carrie, Taylor and many more... I heard your encouragement in my head (*"You should write a book...you could totally do it!"*) and it truly gave me the confidence to start.

Next, Kevin, you spent many hours helping me with a new blog layout because it was my original plan just to post this book chapter by chapter on the blog. I needed somewhere to go to think, so Eileen and Miss Lee, you opened up your *quiet* homes and let me write in your basements. You guys all gave me confidence to keep pursuing this passion.

There were so many of you who helped watch my girls to give me space for this project. Kepley and Garza girls, you were the first ones brave enough to watch them (and my girls are now forever in love with you). Cassandra, Sara, Edith, Becky, Kathy, you have all been so generous to love on my girls and

I am always humbled by your willingness to help (Becky, as I type this, you are in the other room feeding my kids dinner).

Along the way, some of you have been brave enough to read my roughest thoughts and give feedback. Chardonee, you read this and told me that this story needed to be told. Thank you for sending me business cards and a note telling me you believed in me. You'll never know how that small act reignited the fire after I decided the last thing the world needed was another book. Karen and Amanda, you were willing to read and critique and I'm so thankful for you guys.

Linnea, thank you for the hours of reading and editing you've put into this. Your friendship, your support, your gentle pushes have all made this book possible. You have been a consistent cheerleader and I consistently thank God for putting you in my life.

My dear parents, you generously gave me some writing money for babysitters and a writing conference. You'll never know how much of a confirmation that was to keep writing. My amazing in-laws, John and Connie, you were so willing to watch the little ones so I could have a "writing retreat" at your church mission house. Garman family, I love you all. You guys have taught me more than you realize about sacrifice, hard work, and generosity.

Christine, Greg, Willie, Kevin B., Matt, Priscilla, Nate, Laura, Karla, all of my PPW's (and so many more that I couldn't possibly list), you guys have all fed me encouragement that was the fuel to finish. Danielle and Devynn, thank you so much for your work on the cover. The people of Pillar Church, you have prayed for and encouraged me and I am forever grateful for you. I consistently stand in awe of God when I think of the church He has led me to.

Haley Jane, Darcy Elaine, Gracie Kane, and Penelope Raine, you guys have been such cute little supporters on the sidelines. I'm so sorry, Darcy, that I used a **bridge** on the cover instead of a *heart*...I hope you can find it in your heart to forgive me!

Colby John...what can I say? You have been the midwife helping me birth this book and you deserve an award for enduring the longest child-birthing session known to man. You have watched me go back and forth for *years* (five to be exact) about whether or not to write this book. Thanks for loving me even when I'm a pendulum. I'm so thankful God gave you to me.

Jesus, you have carried me every step of the way on this journey and I'm so thankful you gave me the strength to tell about it.

ABOUT THE AUTHOR

Annie is a Midwestern girl who finds herself living in the suburbs of Washington D.C. with her husband and four young girls. She went to Liberty University where she graduated with a degree in Teaching English as a Second Language and met her husband Colby. Annie is passionate about knowing Christ and making Him known in whatever situation she finds herself in. She writes about her adventures being a mother and pastor's wife at **anniebgarman.com**.